G.

Collected Memo...

1895-1939

Liz Forewood

GROWING UP IN WALES

Collected Memories
of Childhood in Wales
1895–1939

edited by
Jeffrey Grenfell-Hill

GOMER

First impression—November 1996

ISBN 1 85902 349 5

Printed in Wales at
Gomer Press, Llandysul, Ceredigion

DEDICATED TO THE MEMORY

of

RUTH GRENFELL 1901—1956

SCHOOL MISTRESS

CONTENTS

ACKNOWLEDGEMENTS

I have been helped in this project by many of my friends. It was in 1979 that I started to record the memories of people I knew. Philip Miles, an undergraduate friend of mine, kindly let me have the record he had made of his father's aunt, Annie Miles, and I corresponded with her for some time. Margaret Kilpatrick introduced me to friends and often read my manuscript. Bill Tonkin was invaluable as a correspondent who was willing to interview octo- and nonagenarians on my behalf. Mrs. Sue Medd of the Glamorgan Family History Society asked members to contribute and kindly gave of her time to help me collect their responses. And I would like to thank all those members of the Gwent and Glamorgan Family History Societies who so generously responded to my plea for their "memories of childhood." Not all their "notes" could be included, but their responses remain central to the archive which I am building up on childhood in Wales and will, I hope, be used again in a more detailed study. My brother Kenneth has taken photographic copies and endlessly reproduced them for me. June Johnson has typed up the manuscript. And last, but not least, I would like to thank my wife Muriel, who supports me in all my literary projects, and who spends a great deal of her time alone.

Childhood: Conversations Recorded

"...oral testimony takes us back to actual experience
and lived differences."

Trevor Lummis, *Listening To History*

Find the key and unlock the door. The memories of childhood, locked away for many of us, can be released into the conscious mind if someone is only curious enough to ask the right questions. Once the 'door' is opened, the sights, smells and emotions are recreated very quickly: the images are sharp and real for us as they were when we were children. And of all our memories, perhaps it is those of childhood which will always be the most easily recollected if given the chance to surface.

The Celts have always been a race ready to talk, to relive life as part of an oral tradition which goes back to our remote past. The telling of tales has always been a potent force in Celtic society and it may well be that for Welsh people today, no less than for their forebears, the ability to retell the past is vital to their present well-being. Certainly for listener or reader, accounts such as those gathered here provide a fascinating dimension to one's knowledge of a particular period, a particular people and the society in which they lived.

In Welsh historiography at present there is little to illuminate what went on at the beginning of this century within the domestic sphere, cut off from public view by walls, doors and curtained windows. Through this collection of memories of growing up in the south Wales valleys and towns, the reader will gain some knowledge of the everyday lives—at home, in school and at work—of people who grew up before the second world war. The themes which emerge from the thirteen full accounts chosen for this book are those we might expect: courtship, birth, domesticity, going to school, community life, and finally, getting a job and back to courtship: they form a recognizable cycle.

How these themes were woven into the pattern of people's lives is amply illustrated by the detailed memories shared by my generous respondents. Together, they give us a picture of a life that in south

9

Wales, as in most of Europe, would be irrevocably changed during the inter-war period.

By way of introduction, it may prove enlightening to work our way through the cycle of childhood and child-rearing in the light of comments and information gleaned from people whose full accounts I have not been able to include. And one good starting point in the cycle which brings forth children is, of course, courtship.

Young men and women of the working classes had more freedom to mix with the opposite sex than those of the middle classes. Being able or having to start work at thirteen or fourteen gave them a certain independence. It allowed them to buy a few attractive clothes, and, as young adults they could demand more time away from the supervision of their family. A curfew for girls operated in most families, and even when bringing home a wage packet, teenage girls had to be home when their fathers expected them: often by 9.30pm. Girls of all classes could expect to meet eligible young men at chapel or church, at concerts, church teas and, of course, when visiting relatives. Middle class daughters had much less freedom, and certainly could not participate in the casual meetings which took place in certain locations in the towns and large villages. David Killa recalls:

> My parents first met at the Middle Gate of Swansea Market as it was called. The year was 1911, and it was customary for young men and women to gather there and to get off with the opposite sex. If they did, they were said to have 'clicked', a term used up to my courting days in the late '30s.

> On the evening my parents met, my mother and her friend noticed two young men at the Middle Gate smiling at them, and the girls who were eating oranges, squeezed the pips between their fingers, and some of them hit one of the young men, who came over to speak to my future mother, and eventually the four of them went to see a show at the nearby Empire Theatre. A year later they were married.

Brenda Hood's father saw her mother scrubbing the front doorstep of her parent's house on Sandy Road, Llanelli one February day in 1919. He had been demobbed from the navy and asked her to go out with him to the pictures. Apparently he had noticed her before when he was home on leave as they both lived with their parents on the same road. Her name was Mary Wooding and she was the daughter of a colliery engine-man. During the war she had worked at the Pembrey Ammunitions Factory. They were both twenty-two and David Hood was a "behinder in the tin-plate works" where his father was also an engine-man. The young couple had a similar background, and so started a courtship. They met at Mary's eldest sister's house and occasionally at the Hood's. When they had been courting three months Mary discovered that she was pregnant and so they got engaged. On the first day of June 1919 they married in the Registry Office and went to live with the Hoods: there was no money for a honeymoon. Six months later Mary had a miscarriage when she discovered her nineteen-year-old sister-in-law dead in bed: the girl had had a heart attack. Mary was so shocked that she fainted and later aborted a baby girl. It was November. During the following January she conceived again, and in September 1921 gave birth to a son. Brenda was born in 1923.

Phyllis Llewellyn, who was born in 1915 maintains that the sons of farmers in the countryside around Pontypridd were not encouraged to get married young as they were needed to work on the farm. They often overcame this by getting their fiancées pregnant, thereby forcing their parents permission for an early marriage.

Girls looked out for young men who would have regular employment, were sober and God-fearing (if possible) with no reputation for being 'wild.' Fathers and brothers usually 'policed' their choice of partners, and made it known if they disapproved. Young men wanted to find a wife who would be a good mother and domestic paragon: capable of living within the allotted housekeeping money *he* decided she should have. The security of their future family would rest not so much on compatibility, but good management from both partners. As soon as a young woman married she was expected to get pregnant if she wasn't so already.

One of my respondents recounted the circumstances of the birth of her only child. I shall call her Mina. She was born in Swansea in 1895 and her father worked at the Cwmfelin Tin Works, while her mother kept a grocery shop in the parlour of their home in Manselton. Mina's parents had eight children, and in order to feed and clothe them all,

11

both worked hard to make some extra money. At first, Mina's mother had sold kippers and bloaters from her parlour shop. However, their landlord offered them a house with a shop front for 5s. a week: she took it and extended her stock, selling groceries, greengroceries and sweets. Mina's father rented two plots of land and grew vegetables for his wife to sell. He also grew herbs which his children tied up in bunches, and he chopped wood into sticks which the children would tie into bundles: herbs and sticks were then sold in the shop. Mina's mother also assisted one of the local midwives as a general nurse when a woman was confined. When Mina's pregnancy was nearing its end, she felt quite confident about the care she would receive.

Mina had been courting a local boy, and when war broke out in 1914 she was nineteen. They married just before he left for France. At the battle of the Somme he was wounded in the neck, face, arm and leg and was the only survivor in his contingent of men. Mina did not get pregnant until 1918 when she was twenty-three: this is what she has to say about giving birth:

> I was quite some time overdue and by this particular Saturday I had been in labour some time. On the Sunday morning my husband came to me and could see my distress. The midwife and my husband and my older brother were very concerned and so a doctor was called. In those days, the midwife was reluctant to call a doctor. She felt it was a personal failure to cope if she had to call the doctor. The doctor was eventually called and then he called another doctor. I was being heavily sedated with chloroform during this time.
>
> By the Sunday night my mother told me that I had had the baby. I was so drugged I could not take it in. On waking on the Monday the midwife told me the baby was dead born. It was a breech birth, and the doctors had broken its neck and leg during delivery.
>
> I also discovered that my legs had been tied at the ankles and the knees after the delivery. I insisted on seeing my baby, which was a boy.
>
> The following day the undertaker came with the tiniest coffin made of oak. He told me that he would bury the baby in a plot reserved for still-born babies at the end of a row of graves next to the boundary wall in Cockett Cemetery. I never knew where my child was buried. That was to be my only child.

The sadness of losing her only child stayed with Mina all her life. Another respondent of the same generation reported that some undertakers would place a still-born baby in the coffin of an adult due for burial. The relatives of the deceased were not aware of this and the parents of the child would not know how the baby had been disposed of: "it was the undertaker's secret." In many families wives gave birth to still-born babies, or their babies died soon after. Untrained midwives did the best they could. It was usual for women to stay in bed following confinement for periods of two to four weeks, depending on whether the confinement had been complicated or not. Due to the long periods of being unable to get any exercise many women developed what was commonly known as 'white leg': caused by poor blood circulation "and was probably a form of blood clotting or thrombosis".

Muriel Black's father, listening to her mother giving birth to her in 1921 decided that his wife "would never have to go through *that* again." And there were no more children. Mrs. Black's labour was long and hard: in the later stages she had to be moved to the bottom of the bed for easier access by the doctor. When the birth was over, she had to remain in the same position for three whole days before being moved. Part of her diet afterwards was "raw minced liver".

Arthur Perry, aged twenty-four and May Jones, aged twenty were married in 1910 at Blaenafon and Edna, their first child was born two years later. May's mother had been widowed early, and her daughter had helped bring up six younger siblings in a home which "bordered on poverty." Arthur Perry's family came originally from Herefordshire, his father was an "overman" in the iron works at Blaenafon, and he went as a fourteen-year-old boy first as a collier but "soon...went into the fitting shop of the colliery" at the "now well-known Big Pit." Edna maintains that not long after her birth in 1912:

> ... my father took a hard look at declining Blaenafon and decided life for a family man needed broader horizons and travelled to Youngstown in Ohio. During the time my father was in America my mother and I lived with my paternal grandfather (grandmother had died) and also my maternal grandmother.
>
> Despite many requests to my mother to move to America, where things

were going well for Dad, she declined and my father eventually returned to Wales when I was one year and eight months old. Job prospects in Blaenafon were even worse than when he left, but coastal Port Talbot had a brighter future and my father prospering on his American experience took work as an electrician in what was then Baldwin's Steelworks, virtually in the middle of Port Talbot.

Port Talbot was to become their home. One can see that this Welsh woman showed an independence of spirit and despite repeated calls to join a husband in Ohio, refused to leave Wales. The Perry family are indicative of the smaller, more companionable family which seemed to be developing in the Twenties. There were significant gaps between the births of their children, Edna in 1912, followed by a brother in 1915 and another (their last child) in 1920.

Some of my respondents had no idea what their fathers earned. However, a few could remember precisely. Thomas John Protheroe, born in 1899, the son of Thomas John Protheroe who was a haulier with the horses in a colliery at Ynyswen said his father earned £1.18s.0d. a fortnight. Thomas George Steadman, born in 1903, thought that his father earned £2.10s.0d. a week as a colliery sawyer. The welfare of the family was much improved if father kept an allotment. Pigs were much favoured in the mining communities, as was the keeping of hens. Some men could always be relied upon to catch a rabbit or two for the pot. Esau Alexander, born in 1919 had a father who was a colliery winder bringing home £1.5s.0d. a week. His wife Jennifer had ten children between 1905 and 1921 (and twin girls in 1930 when she was fifty-one). It was essential for her husband and older boys to catch wild animals for the pot. They lived at Cadle, three miles outside Swansea:

> Father had a shotgun and twice or so a week he'd go out to shoot rabbits and snipe. The snipe would be boiled and used the following day for him to take to work. All we boys went fishing—with a bent pin shaped into a hook, cotton and a stick, then a worm—and caught trout and eels: when we caught something it was a meal. Me and Emlyn my brother were good with our catapults and caught water fowl—moorhens—we'd stalk them along the river and into the woods.

Whatever the size of the wage packet it was the role of the wife to see that she managed on what was doled out to her, usually on a Saturday morning, or late afternoon if she was unfortunate to have a husband who went to the pub first. This is why shops stayed open so late on Saturdays.

The good housewife made her own jams, pickles, chutneys and preserved as much fruit as she could in season. Hilda Evans growing up in St. Thomas, Swansea in the early 1900s remembers that "it was the custom in the area for women to make their own dough and take the dough in a loaf tin to the bakery to be baked." The local baker was also used at Christmas time. Ellen May Roberts' mother in Trelewis made six plum puddings, four *Bara Brith* and a rich fruit cake which were all taken to the baker's in the village to be baked and collected at the end of the day. Louise Currie in Abercynon can remember seeing "the little parade of mothers carrying" at Christmas time "the birds, all stuffed, across the road to Mr. Evans' bakehouse where these birds were cooked. The smell in the road was so appetizing." But Lorna Lockett as a little girl in Rhydycar in 1922 remembers that her mother cooked her own Christmas goose: "in the front of the fire hanging from a jack with the goose grease dripping into a meat tin, which was afterwards put into jars and kept for throat and chest problems." Megan Jones' mother in Pencoed also put her bird on a revolving spit, but when she had a new range put in later, could use the oven. "When mothers sent their weekly bread to the baker he would put a skewer with a numbered disc in the dough to identify which loaf belonged to which family." Edna Perry also recalls that "breakfast was always porridge or bread and tea—we called that *slops*—the bread was soaked in hot tea with sugar. Dinner was always soups or stews." The main meal in most homes was eaten at midday and children were expected to carry dinners to their fathers or grandfathers who were working.

Muriel Black, born in 1921, the daughter of William Black, remembers going with her mother's youngest sister into the Cwmfelin Steel Works with her grandfather's midday meal:

> The food could be hot or cold, it depended. The works were near where we lived in Cwmbwrla. I was quite small and we went right into the works and up onto the stage with the food, where the huge furnaces were,

and where the men would sit to have their food. Tadcu would ask us to sing or recite for them. He was a happy jovial little man.

Lilian Jones went to Brynmill School, Swansea, where they seemed not to be too strict about her being on time for the afternoon session. Her teacher knew that each dinner-time Lilian had to take her father his meal:

> In the dinner hour at school it was my daily job to take Dada his dinner. I was probably twelve by then. It would mean running down Westbury Street to our house at 22, King Edward Road, getting from my mother a basin with meat and gravy—well wrapped in newspaper to keep it hot—and another basin with vegetables. Then there was a serviette wrapped around the bread—and a knife, fork and dinner plate. Then I'd run to catch the tram to take me to Alexandra Road where my father worked as a florist and fruiterer. I'd wait for him to have dinner and bring back the empty basins and dirty plate. When I got back home I'd manage to have my own dinner—then make a dash for school. I was nearly always late in the afternoon. There didn't seem to be a big fuss about my always being late. They must have realised my father needed his dinner.

Norman Church, born in 1907, the son of Robert Church, lived in Newport and when his father was working a Sunday shift would be sent with his dinner to the Orb Works: he went inside to where he knew his father would be amongst the "massive machinery used in steel making."

Contrary to popular opinion some men in Wales were involved in the daily routine of the household and helped their wives as best they could. With full employment and allotments to work on there was not much time left over. Brenda Hood's father, David "was a really good cook, especially dinners and milk puddings." Brenda never remembers her mother cooking a Sunday dinner or the midday meal in the week when her father worked an afternoon shift. Joseph Fullard, too, confirmed that his father, William, "made Sunday dinner." Sarah Bowen, whose father was a miner in Merthyr Tydfil said he "often helped with domestic chores, but behind closed doors of course".

Women worked hard in the industrial areas to keep their homes clean, fighting the daily conditions which brought factory fumes and coal dust into their houses. Miriam Hagedon born in 1896 in Loughor remembers that the only mat they had, was a coconut one in front of the fire. The rest of the floor was strewn with sand which was swept up once a week and heated in an old tin over the fire to clean it and get the lumps out of it. Most roads were dust-tracks and boots brought in a lot of dirt. It was a constant battle. In the evenings women spent their time in darning and mending. Daughters were expected to help their mothers as much as possible.

For those who were slightly better off, help was to be had. Ellen May Roberts, born in 1911, (with two sisters and two brothers), was the eldest daughter of a colliery fireman. Her mother was able to have a char lady in once a week, sent her washing out to be laundered, had the girls help her in the house, and their father always cleaned their boots and shoes.

The welfare of the family was very much a mother's concern. And central to washing, cooking and keeping warm was the fire. Whatever happened, the fire had to be kept going at all costs. Coal had to be eked out so that there was always sufficient in the coal house to light the fire. Even the wives of colliers had to be careful in their use of coal. Adelaid Rule, born in 1909, grew up in Ammanford, and it was her job to make *pele* to supplement the burning of the coal itself:

> It was my job to break up the coal when it came from the colliery. Some of it would flake away; it fell into small bits. This would be kept to one side to make into *pele*: these were round balls made of clay and coal for burning in the fire. A hole would be dug in the garden, the ground was made up of clay; we'd dig up one bucket of clay, and this would be mixed with six buckets of small coal. The hole would gather water from the garden, so the clay was moist. I had to spend some time treading the clay and coal together, working it together with my boots until the consistency was right. After this I had to mould the great slab into lumps. It took a lot of time, and hard work; it would have been constantly turned and moved around (like making pastry) until it was ready to be made up. When all of it was done, I'd make it into balls, these were then put in a corner of the coal shed, where they dried out, ready for use. The *pele* got red–hot in the grate, they made a lot of heat. Later on we used cement to bind it all together. But when I was a girl, it was always clay from the garden: and it was tough on the feet in big boots.

The coal mixed with *pele* was essential for the big weekly wash which universally took place after the sabbath day. In most homes Monday was Wash Day. It was the day when mother slaved over the laundry. Some women had older daughters to help; some paid a washer-woman to come in; while those with domestic servants left the whole laborious process to others. Early on Monday morning the copper boiler would be filled with water and the fire lit in the brick fireplace underneath the boiler. Caroline Lockman remembers it all well:

> When the water was hot enough, it would be transferred to the wash tub and pummelled with the wooden 'dolly.' The 'dolly' was a long handled sort of stool with legs, that was raised and lowered in the tub to activate the water. This required strong arms and plenty of muscle power. All the white clothes had to be boiled separately, then rinsed thoroughly and then a final rinse in the water to which the blue bag was immersed to give the clothes a sparkling white look. Then there were some items which required starching before ironing. You can imagine the load for seven of us. Wash day was a long hard stint.

Louise Currie, born in 1911, the daughter of David Currie a colliery official, remembers that her mother's washing extended over three days. Mrs. Currie, from the time of her marriage had a baby every eighteen months "until the last three when she had a few years in between." Her first two children had died soon after birth, and she was to later "bury an eighteen-month-old little girl." In all, she had thirteen births, and raised ten children: six boys and four girls. They lived in Abercynon. Mrs. Currie, was unusual in her neighbourhood for having been born in the United States of America and brought to Wales when she was eighteen by her parents who had earlier emigrated. She was lucky enough to afford a woman to help her with the washing. On Mondays "all the white linen was boiled and starched. Tuesdays all the coloured clothes were washed. On Wednesdays the working clothes. There was a big iron mangle with large wooden rollers" to help squeeze out the excess water. After the wash:

> There came the damping down of the starched linen, and all the ironing with flat irons heated on the fire, wiped and placed in a metal shield.

Mary Thomas's sister, who was sixteen years older than her, "did all the washing" for her mother. This must have considerably eased the strain on Mrs. Thomas who had nine children. Mary was the seventh, and born in 1919. Her father, William Thomas, was a tin-plate worker who was often out of work in the 1920s. He would leave home and look for work. However, in 1922 he answered an advertisement in the local evening paper in which an American Company was advertising for workers to go out to India. William got a job with them and left Briton Ferry on a three year contract. Mrs. Thomas and the children did not see him again until the three years were up in 1925 and he returned home on a six month leave of absence. While he was at home he told them that he would be returning to Calcutta. It was decided that his wife, their daughter Mary and her younger brother would join him there. The older children were to be left with their grandparents. When the three of them left Briton Ferry it was the start of a great adventure and a new life:

There was great excitement preparing for the journey to India. We stayed overnight in Tilbury before boarding the ship to start a five week journey. Father was waiting on the quayside in Calcutta to meet us when we disembarked. After the lean times in Briton Ferry it was rather grand to find we had a nurse to help mother with the children and the chores.

Life was so different in India and we did not have to go to school. Mother gave us lessons every day in reading, writing and sums.

One day father took us for a walk in the jungle when a snake fell from a tree onto his arm.

Another incident I remember was getting lost in the jungle and mother and the servant coming to find us. The monsoon season was frightening and yet exciting to experience. Unfortunately, we had to return home after two years because I had malaria in 1928. I remember my grandparents and my older brothers meeting us at the station on our return. It was back to the bad old days again. Father could not get work and life changed completely for me. When I went back to school I won a prize for doing well: so my mother did a good job at teaching us.

When we lived in Calcutta my mother received such a good housekeeping allowance I remember her saying she wished she could stay in India for ever.

Having sufficient housekeeping money was a problem for many women. The situation could be alleviated somewhat if sons and daughters could help. Many children found paid jobs of one sort or another which could be done before going to school. Joseph Fullard living in Pontypool found one when he was twelve: it meant going to the station by 7.30am. where he waited for a train to deliver crates of fruit and vegetables. When they were taken off the train he loaded them onto a station "wheelbarrow" and delivered them to Mrs. Price's shop. For this job she gave him tuppence and a few apples which he "proudly" took home to his mother. He had to return the "wheelbarrow" before going on to school. Violet May Lewis living in Pontypridd used to pod the peas in the backyard of a local 'Faggots and Peas' shop. She also went to the local butchers and cleaned out the intestines of a slaughtered pig before they were cooked and sold as "chitterlings." Women made extra money paper-hanging for neighbours, and some made toffee-apples to sell from their kitchen.

The smaller the house the easier it was to keep warm. House sizes, of course, varied considerably. Some were "one up, one down." Many in Morriston near Swansea were built early on in the industrialization of the area. Thomas Rabey, who had a brother and sister and whose father George worked in the tin-plate works, recalled a house they rented on Cwmbath Road:

> It consisted of one bedroom which led straight onto the stairs with no door. There was one living room which also served as a washroom and kitchen. There was no drain or sink. It had a coal-fire range with an oven. Below this room was a cellar where the coal was kept. There was an outside lavatory shared with another family and water had to be carried down to it so we could flush it. Across the road we had a fair-sized garden.

The death of a mother could mean the dispersal of the family. When Violet May Lewis's mother died in 1917 of cancer (she was only twenty-eight) she left four motherless children behind and a badly wounded father who had only just survived the Battle of the Somme in the previous year and was still in a military hospital. There were two girls, Gwladys who was eight, Violet who was only six, Glyndwr five, and the 'baby' Gwilym not yet three. On a July day they followed their mother's coffin "up to the mountain cemetery" and threw posies of doe daisies into the grave. Later, when the mourners had left, one boy was taken by their mother's sister and later the other by their paternal grandmother. The two girls were put into an orphanage in Staffordshire for the first three years before being sent to the Swansea Orphan Home where the orphans were known as 'The Ministry of Pensions Children.' For girls in an orphanage at this time there was very little option but to be trained for domestic service at fifteen. May was not happy about this:

> I resented this somewhat as I felt my education was at a standstill—no books available. We were always expected to be busy either knitting or sewing. There was a schoolroom in the orphanage where one Governess taught the lot of us from four to sixteen years. How she coped with us all I do not know.
>
> Life changed in 1921-22 when a new matron came with new ideas. A very gifted woman. She worked hard to raise money for the children's holiday fund and each year we went to Horton, Gower, for five to six weeks. In October 1924 the children of school age were allowed to join St. Helen's School. This was a great step forward. However, I was one of the unfortunate ones as I was fourteen in the December and was not accepted just for the two months. So I became a 'House Girl': in training for service and looking after babies of twelve months to five years. Sometimes we thought we were very 'hard done by', but we were happy and never lonely. When I was sixteen I became a member on the staff, starting as 'kitchen assistant' and worked my way up to being deputy-matron by the time I left at thirty-six.
>
> But I often wished I had had a better schooling.

Muriel Powell, born in 1915, the daughter of a telegraphist, Thomas Powell, was brought up in a spacious house on King Edward Road, Swansea, with its own separate bathroom. Their newspaper boy had one leg shorter than the other and never wore shoes or stockings: barefooted children were a common sight. Muriel went to Brynmill Infants School which was a mixture of children from prosperous and poor homes: one of three girls, their mother would regularly wash their hair in *Life Buoy* soap to try and keep their heads free of lice. There seemed to be "a lot of hungry children around" and some, calling for Muriel in the morning, would start to cry because they had not been given any breakfast, and Mrs. Powell would feed them. Muriel's father had been orphaned at an early age, and so his aunt, the headmistress of York School brought him up: she, too, lived with her nephew's family:

> As mother's arthritis grew worse our Aunt Mary would do things to help groom us. She would brush our hair and we girls would sit beside her whilst she gave us a manicure: having been a headmistress she was very particular of our appearance. Mother had been a good machinist and made all our dresses. She had been trained as a dressmaker and so was able to make all our clothes. There was always a Whitsun dress and probably dresses whenever we needed them.
>
> As a retired headmistress it was Aunt Mary who set the standards. Teachers did in those days.

★　★　★

Every community had its local schools. In the towns and villages, compulsory education played a significant part in the lives of the local children and the standard they achieved can be seen when the reader comes to the letters Ernest Grenfell and Alice Taylor wrote to each other in the 1890s. Both writers were educated at the local elementary school which would have on its staff both certificated and uncertificated teachers as well as pupil teachers. Many families in the late Victorian and Edwardian years hoped to train at least one daughter as a teacher. For both working and middle class girls teaching offered them the chance to have a profession.

In the heavily populated valleys of south Wales the loss of male teachers who went to be soldiers in the war years 1914–1918 opened up significant job prospects for young women of seventeen. The Great War brought into the teaching profession nationally, 13,000 more women. Girls went off to colleges such as the Glamorgan Training College in Swansea with high hopes. Annie Miles and Ruth Grenfell were there at the same time. However, by the time they were trained teachers and looking for jobs in 1921, marriage and teaching in south Wales could not be combined. Both chose teaching.

Local Authorities introduced the marriage bar as an antidote to the economic crisis of 1921: they refused to appoint women as teachers, forced them to resign on marriage and dismissed those who were married. By 1926 three quarters of Local Education Authorities operated a marriage bar. In south Wales with its high male unemployment rates in the 1920s and 30s, the Education Committees must have felt justified in victimising women. If they wanted to remain teachers they had to remain single. Such was the hostility at the thought of married women teachers and their husbands enjoying a double income. In a region where there was no tradition of high married female employment (as a result of its heavy industry), the idea of double incomes was anathema. A seventeen-year-old Welsh girl had to be very sure of her career choice in such a climate of forced spinsterhood.

When talking about schooldays some of my respondents looked back with an obvious sense of nostalgia that may have coloured their memory. After all, 'the best days of your life' can seem so after a lapse of well over fifty years. The responses were, as one might expect, varied. For some there is a tendency to claim it was clouting, caning and misery. Some were ambivalent. The truth, for what it's worth, may be that schooldays in the past are very much as they are now: a series of good days and bad days, peopled by teachers of a diversity which precludes one from thinking in terms of stereotypes.

Joyce Leakey, born in 1921, the daughter of Alexander Leakey was first of all sent to Brynhyfryd Infants School, Swansea:

> But it was strict, so very strict. I broke my heart going and only went for a few weeks, then my mother kept me home because they would slap and hit the children: even in the Babies Class.

Eventually Mrs. Leakey sent Joyce to Manselton Infants School instead:

> That school was completely different. The headmistress of the Infants was Miss Atkins, a lady: she never even shouted.
> We had slates and chalk for letters. Printing letters, but no connecting up at first. There was singing. Simple arithmetic.
> There was drawing. Then we used pencil on paper. We were taught to make a body, faintly in joints, all the limbs as moving joints. They taught us to think in terms of limbs and then afterwards they would make us dress it. It made us all think a lot about movement. The teacher would tell us to make the body look as if it was flying a kite, or jumping or bending down.

We made spill boxes for paper lighters: a square of parchment-like paper, with raffia around the edges. We did a lot of raffia work I can tell you! Making table-mats or little boxes and crosses. Decorations, too, with dried flowers worked into a design.

On May Day we all danced around a May Pole.

When she was twenty-eight in 1929 Ruth Grenfell joined the staff of Dyfatty Infants School in Swansea. It was located in the north of the town, close to some of the poorest districts. The school log books give a detailed account of the day-to-day activities of an infants school, even noting that on November 11th, 1920 the two minute silence was observed in order to commemorate the Armistice of 1918. Nurse Jones visited regularly for the "Hair Parade" to see if the children had nits. The headteacher moaned about the fact that Sunday School treats taken on schooldays kept the children away. Because it served the Catholic community there was a half day holiday on St. Patrick's Day, as well as the usual celebrations for St. David's Day. On Empire Day, May 24th, 1927 there were "playlets, songs and recitations on *Our Empire*." As a teenager, Ruth's youngest sister Alys remembers her sister's anxieties for the children at Dyfatty:

Ruth was heartbroken some days at the poor state of the children. Coming from homes with next to nothing. Poor bedraggled things. Some never even had handkerchiefs, nothing like that. And runny noses. So she would take some in. She kept a comb, too, to try and comb out the girls' hair, and had bits of ribbon to give them, to try and make them feel better. Matted hair they would have. Some were very badly kept. One little boy walked to school once with both legs in the same trouser leg: crossed a busy road, walking like that. He'd either had to dress himself or his mother hadn't bothered properly. Some had no macs, nothing to keep them dry on wet days. They came to school soaking wet. And a lot of them on their own.

Ruth worried so much about the infants crossing the road. There had been nasty accidents. It was so busy. They would put their coats on, well, if they were lucky to have a coat, and then she made them wait until they were all ready, and then she took them in a file down the road and saw to it that they all crossed safely. She worried all the time about them.

Many children in the rural areas walked a considerable distance to school. Maud Rosser who started school when she was five in 1902 walked one and a half miles to Penllergaer, carrying her midday meal. Sometimes she and her brother Blais would 'mitch' school in order to help their father on his greengrocery round. When their headmaster Mr. Jenkins caught them he would say:

There we are then, little and good like a Welshman's cow.

Jenkin David, born in 1900, the son of William David, a stonemason lived in Efail-Fach. Pontrhydyfen, and walked to Ton Mawr Church School. He also took sandwiches and "a small tea-caddy" filled with tea for his dinner which he used to have "in an old ladies house in Parkers Row" so he wouldn't have to walk all the way home and back again for the afternoon session. He started school at five-years-old and the first thing he learned was to add up "using coloured beads".

Trevor Wilde, born in 1913, went to Aberbeeg School near Abertillery and although he believes "for an elementary level the school standard was good" he does remember an incident of very unfair treatment by the headmaster which illustrates the political tensions in the mining communities of Monmouthshire:

Discipline was high, and bordered at times on cruelty. I was seated at an end desk one day, and the headmaster, Mr. Martindale, a very big man, came down the aisle. I was writing, and my index finger was crooked on top of the pen. He saw it, and as he always insisted that the finger should be laid flat down the length of the pen, reacted at the sight. I felt a fist hard in my back, and then I was sprawling in the aisle gasping for breath at the punch. The real reason wasn't anything to do with my finger: it was really a political one. My father attended the local Labour Club. The headmaster was a Conservative. Now, each boy in his turn, when he reached Standard VI, had to go to the Conservative Club at 11.30. each morning and retrieve three flagons of beer for the headmaster. My father knew this happened. And he instructed me that when my turn came round, I was to refuse. Which is what I did. That then, was my punishment.

Brenda Hood, born in 1923, the daughter of David Hood of Pontarddulais, used to look forward to the Cookery and Domestic classes because:

I used to enjoy washing the doll baby with the teacher looking on, because I knew what to do, having had to help my mother with the youngest, who I used to nurse the old Welsh way, with a shawl.

Most schools had to put up with truanting. The Board Man would be sent to their homes to find out where they were. Brenda recalls that:

My brother used to play truant, to go and play on the old coal tip and slide down on an old zinc sheet. Of course, with a lot of other boys. He was always having hidings with my father who was a good, but strict, man.

Esau Alexander who attended Cadle School in the 1920s truanted regularly:

I thought I was a duffer: not able to get on with my lessons. So I'd truant. One time I said my stud had come through the sole of my boot: they'd accept that. I'd truant on average twice a week. If the Board man came to report my absence my mother would not tell my father: in a way she condoned my mitching. Mother didn't set great store by school.

When Brenda Hood was in school in the early 1930s she joined the *Urdd Gobaith Cymru* movement and took part in country dancing and physical training. When the *Urdd Eisteddfod* came to Llanelli she took part in it before the Prince of Wales. However the day is memorable because of an incident which involved a child she used to nurse for 6d. a week:

I will never forget that day, dressed up in my Urdd regalia. I went for a walk up to the dam that had been built by all us kids for swimming a bit, higher up than Banc-y-Bo, near the colliery alongside the railway. And to show off my clothes I went down to where all my friends were gathered. While I was chatting I happened to look down into a part of the river that had gone into a pool and what I thought was a lot of clothing. Naturally, I got interested, and when I went to pull it out—it was a child—I got it out and worked on it just a little—turned it over and found that it was Graham Price, Will and Celia's little boy. His cousin Glenys had taken him for a walk because I had gone to the Urdd Festival and put him to dangle his feet into the water and then left him. He must have toppled in. Good thing that I was there. I saved him. But I had the fault. So I wasn't allowed to go near him for a while anyway.

Daughters were involved in childcare in some way or another. They could also be sent to relatives on a permanent or temporary basis. When Maud Rosser's grandfather eventually sold his foundry in Loughor he went out to the United States of America as a pattern maker. His wife had refused to go with him, and so, at the age of nine or ten, Maud was sent to live with her grandmother in Swansea. It was probably in 1907 and the family did not want Maud's grandmother to live alone. Mr. Rosser senior stayed in America for four to five years and upon his return from New York bought a house in Carmarthen where he and his wife went to live: Maud was then free to return home and her old school.

★　★　★

Most people could not take holidays. Some were lucky if they managed a day trip to Barry Island or Porthcawl. Most made do with the Sunday School outing. But the professional and middle classes could go to the pleasant resorts dotted around Wales. Bessie Higgs, whose father was an elementary school headteacher and had lost his wife in the 'flu epidemic of 1918, usually sent his daughters away on holiday:

> Usually we went for two weeks to Llandrindod Wells with two frumpy old maids who were schoolmistresses. We would go into an apartment consisting of a sitting-room and two bedrooms. We went out to buy our food every day and the landlady cooked it and served it to us in the sitting-room. I hated it because of the frumps. And there was nothing to interest a young girl. Our father—Dada—never came. It was our holiday with chaperones. They went *everywhere* with us.
>
> One year we went to Ross-on-Wye: somewhere different I suppose. One evening we went out on the green and my sister, Gwladys, was horribly bitten by gnats. Still in an apartment, of course, but next door to a pub. These two old maids liked a glass of cider with their meals and Gwladys (she was older than me) would be sent with a jug to get it filled.
>
> Before Mama died in 1918 we went for a month's holiday every summer to a Cann uncle who farmed at Chumleigh in Devon. Dada came too and helped out on the farm. We would cross by paddle steamer from Swansea to Ilfracombe, then go by train to South Molton Road. Then mother's uncle came with a pony and trap to meet us: the highlight of the holiday was trotting through the lanes out to his farm.

27

Muriel Powell, born in 1905, the daughter of Thomas Powell, a telegraphist in Swansea was taken to Ilfracombe or Llandrindod Wells. Sometimes they went to Bath so that her mother could take the baths for her arthritis and they usually stayed for two weeks. If they went to Llandrindod they were all, two brothers and three sisters, made to drink the waters.

Although holidays away from home were too expensive, most families could afford a day trip. These were very popular, especially the day trip aboard the steamer to Ilfracombe which sailed out of Briton Ferry and Swansea. Jenkin David who was living in Efail-Fach, Pontrhydyfen, went with his parents to Ilfracombe once a year. There were also day trips to Porthcawl and Mumbles by pony and trap. When he was older, probably around 1910, the Davids travelled by horse drawn brake which had to be stabled for about half an hour at Neath for food and water. For Norman Church, living in Newport, there were occasional trips to the lighthouse or Goldcliff, about six miles from where he lived "and the nearest point to any sea." It was just a "little expanse of mud and sand" and they travelled by horse-drawn brake along roads "not being tarred but full of dust".

Children were taught to think ahead, to employ thrift, and to save their money. Parents took it upon themselves to instil those virtues which they had learned from their parents: 'strict' was a word used often to describe both parents and teachers. Lena Harris, born in 1898 in Abertillery, the daughter of William Harris a colliery examiner, was usually taken on a fortnight's holiday to Swansea Bay. They would stay in a lodging house. Each day the children were given 6d. as pocket money. One day it was decided to go by bus[1] to a park. There the children spent all day. Lena spent the sixpence in the park. When it was time to return to the lodging house her mother asked Lena and her brother if they had their bus fare. When they said they had spent it, their mother made the conductor put the two children off the bus and they had to walk back.

After school and in the holidays children played out of doors. For girls there was hopscotch, rounders, bat and catty, spinning tops, hoop-

[1] Lena said it was a bus, but it was more likely to have been a tram, or even the Mumbles train as the event took place around 1908.

la, skipping, oranges and lemons and ring-a-ring-a-rosie. Boys played rugby, football, bull rag, catty and dog, marbles, whip and top, five stones and weak donkeys and strong horses. Some of these were more popular before the 1914-18 war, while others were played throughout the period. Working class children had an active life out of doors with their friends.

Wilfred Ellis Roberts, born in 1922 and growing up in Trelewis can remember "great summer days" on the mountainside: "up we would go to White Brook, a pretty spot and make a tent, having got flour sacks from our local bakery and then purchased 2d. worth of small beer from Mrs. Watkins in the village—made from nettles—we had sandwiches—and spend all day trying to catch trout, or playing cricket".

However, on a Sunday, most parents forbade their children to disturb the Sabbath and 'playing outside' was frowned upon. Indoors some parents would not permit games and encouraged reading. There was to be no sewing, knitting or darning. Most of the preparations for Sunday dinner were done on Saturday. Most children attended the chapel services even if some parents did not.

For many children in Wales the life of the chapel was central to their day-to-day existence. Brenda Hood of Pontardulais had a headteacher who was also a deaconess at their local Tabernacle Baptist Chapel. Brenda would take part in the quarterly meetings when she and other children recited, played the piano, read or sang a song: if you were "very good you were asked to take part at the evening service." Brenda and her friends went to chapel every Monday night to attend a class called *Urdd Y Seren Fore* where they learned the Old and New Testament stories and once a year sat an examination called *The Arholiad*. This chapel culture nurtured values and interests in generations of children growing up in Wales.

For some families, music was central to their well-being, and also bolstered their status within the community. George Steadman, who was the son of the landlord of The Ivy Bush Hotel at Pontardawe, came from a family who had originated in Hereford. As a boy, George had been in the choir at St. Peter's Church. When he grew older he was noted for possessing "an exceptionally high-pitched tenor voice" and used to entertain the patrons of The Ivy Bush with his favourite songs: *Come to me Flora, Starboard Watch,* and *Comrades in Arms.* In 1913 the vicar of Pontardawe appointed him as choir master to the newly built St. Mary's at Ynysmeudw near Godregraig about one mile outside Pontardawe, where he lived with his family and worked as a sawyer in the colliery. He had married Eleanor Rosser from Glais near Clydach. One of their sons, Arthur, won the 1918 boys solo under 13 years at the National Eisteddfod in Neath; he had "come first in a hundred voices" and the same day his sister was awarded "a semi-national certificate." All three of the Steadman children were musical: Thomas George, who had been born in 1903, was also a chorister:

> When my father was at home he liked to play the organ. We as a family would group around: a choir all on our own. Our neighbour, Mrs. Thomas, living alone, was so thrilled with our church music that she used to knock at the next door wall, and when my mother would send me to enquire what was the matter, she said: she would like to be entertained by us to spend her Sunday evening.

Some boys did not go to chapel willingly. Jenkin David was one. When he was four in 1904 the Religious Revival was at its height in south Wales and it must have been tedious for a small boy to sit through the long and crowded services which took place. Jenkin's father spent what spare time he had reading his Bible in order to prepare for the chapel meetings held in the evenings. In the David household all food which could be prepared ahead of time was made ready on Saturday as the Sabbath was kept as a Holy Day: even his father's shaving was done on Saturday, rather than Sunday morning. On Monday all their Sunday clothes were brushed and boots cleaned ready for chapel the following weekend. Chapel clothes were usually in dark colours so that they could be worn at a time of mourning.

Maud Rosser remembers that even when she was "very young" her mother used to insist that she accompanied her when she was called to a house to 'lay-out' the dead. Mrs. Rosser was one of the local women in Loughor who could be called upon by relatives to get the body ready for burial. She told Maud that although she might object, one day she would have to do it herself. And child that she was "she had to go".

Tragedy hit Lorna Lockett's family in 1925 when her father was killed, leaving a wife and three children. Killed by "a fall of roof in the Lucy Drift." Lorna was only ten-years-old:

> His body was brought home and the coal dust was washed off him before the undertaker brought his coffin. He remained at home until the funeral even though the cottage was very small. Me, being a girl, was sent to stay with a neighbour. But my elder brother although only eight went to the cemetery in a dark suit and stiff collar. Women did not go to the cemetery: they stayed at home and prepared a meal for the return of the men. The men ate first, then the women, then the neighbours would come. All blinds would be drawn on all windows. There would be a service at the house: women inside and the men standing outside. The singing at such a time was something to be remembered for ever. There would be a hearse and one car for the mourners. All the rest of the men would walk behind the cortege all the way to Cefn Cemetery.

Mourning was strictly regulated: black was worn for three months, then grey, followed by mauve. Families were expected to keep "very much to themselves for a while" after the funeral. The corpse was laid out in the best room, usually the front parlour, and neighbours were expected to call and see the deceased. When Dyfrig Jones' parents married in July 1927, a relative of his mother's had recently died and so her wedding dress had to be in semi-mourning: "it was shades of lavender, pink and silver grey and *not* a wedding gown but a smart, fashionable dress of the era." As Dyfrig's father was an electrical engineer he could afford to take his bride on honeymoon and they went to Ilfracombe, a much favoured destination for so many Welsh 'trippers'.

The children of farmers had very little, if not any, time for leisure activities. Sons and daughters were expected to be fully involved in the running of the farm, although daughters usually helped with the domestic chores. Elizabeth Hannah Beynon, born in 1899, was the daughter of Thomas Beynon of Long Oaks Farm in Penmaen, Gower, a prosperous farmer with 210 acres. She washed dishes, helped with the cooking and "baked bread in a brick oven" which was later used to

31

bake yeast cake in the remaining heat. Elizabeth had to carry water half a mile to the farmhouse for cooking and drinking, but they had water butts to supply them with water for the dishes. She had to feed the chickens, gather eggs, and at Christmas time helped "to kill the chickens and feather them." Floors had to be regularly scrubbed: they were sanded because the men came in with muddy boots." Elizabeth made cheese and butter. When she did have an opportunity to sit down she used the time to crochet. Her parents bought a piano and from the age of twelve she had piano lessons. When she was fourteen, in 1912, she became the organist at Parkmill Chapel. For Elizabeth life centred around the farm, school and chapel, where there were plays which she acted in and *eisteddfodau* in which she recited poetry—her favourite poem was *The Titanic*. They watched the seasons pass by, and after the hay harvest each year Thomas Beynon took his family to Llandrindod Wells for a holiday. At Christmas time they killed one of their own geese: "usually it would be the biggest one as no-one would want to buy it." For Elizabeth life was very much centred on the farm: she rarely went further than Parkmill.

> I only went to town, that's Swansea, at Christmas time, as there was no spare cash to spend and we had a dressmaker to the house for six weeks of the year at 1s.6d. a week. She lived in and worked from 9am. until 7pm. My mother always went in beforehand and bought the cloth from Thomas Lewis of Oxford Street, Swansea. We would choose the pictures from Weldones fashion book, then we would buy the patterns by sending away for them. The dressmaker would then know what to do. All my underwear was white calico, all my summer frocks would be white cotton, which would be washed, starched and ironed, so they would be kept fresh looking. Winter frocks were made from Welsh flannel, overcoats also from Welsh flannel because it was warm. My favourite colours were blue and brown because I had auburn hair.

When Elizabeth left school at fourteen the First World War "broke out" and so she had "to work for King and Country." She had to do "outside work" like the women in the Land Army, mobilised to take the place of the men who had left the farms to fight in the war. Elizabeth's father disliked having to accept women workers on his farm.

There were farmers who encouraged the local children to come out to their fields when the hay was being gathered in and Louise Currie at Abercynon would go with her friends "to the farms at hay-making time." It was thought "great fun" to be "tossing the hay by hand. Lots of children took part and had a lovely tea afterwards in the fields." This way traditional links with the countryside were maintained.

Welsh couples who had emigrated in the nineteenth century to the United States of America to farm, sometimes returned to Wales. One couple left older children behind. When Louise Currie's maternal grandparents returned from America after emigrating there in the last quarter of the nineteenth century, they settled in Abercynon. Louise remembers being told that they had returned because 'they wanted to die in their own country.' Her grandparents had opened a general shop which her grandmother continued to run after her husband's death. Louise and the rest of the family moved in to live with their grandmother so that she would not be on her own. When the strikes hit the south Wales valleys Louise maintains that her Grandma Rees in 1921:

> . . . gave families credit when the Co-operative shops would not let their customers have anything above £5 credit. My darling mother told Grandma she would have nothing left—but I'll never forget her answer—"I cannot see the poor people starve." When she died soon after, the shop was closed. Not a penny was paid back, but those folk went back to the Co-op when the strike was over.
>
> My mother always grieved about the fact that she was torn away from her older brothers and sisters and brought back to Wales. She was not quite eighteen when it happened and her sister Edith was about sixteen: so back to Wales they had to go protesting: to look after their parents in their old age I guess. My mother even tried to run away at the dockside but grandpa caught her. Eventually they arrived at Liverpool docks.
>
> Because our mother had grown up on a farm in the U.S.A. she knew how to cure skins. She made a goatskin rug for our parlour and cured rabbit skins to make us muffs.
>
> She never forgot that her father forced her to go back to Wales with him.

★　　★　　★

Fathers had a great deal of power over their children, and especially their daughters. There is no clearer evidence of this than the jobs they found upon leaving school. Muriel Powell, who grew up in a middle class family in Swansea was told exactly what she would be:

> As we approached school leaving age—and we girls were at the Convent School then—our father arranged what we should do. We had no choice or say in the matter whatsoever. My elder sister Gwennie went into the office of father's friend Mr. Purser the solicitor. I was sent into the Post Office as a probationer and later became a telephonist (that was my father's wish). Our sister Edna was kept at home to help our mother—there was no thought given to a job for *her*. Mother's *help* Edna was going to be.

If parents could afford it, they apprenticed daughters as seamstresses, or dressmakers, so that they could make their own and childrens clothes after they married. Having been trained to cut out and make clothes properly, their children could be fitted out with decent looking clothes for just the cost of the material. In this process, a sewing machine was essential and all those women who could afford it had one. Mrs. Carrie Lockman who had four daughters and a son to clothe, was fortunate that she had been trained as a seamstress. Her children were considered so well-dressed that they were labelled as 'posh' and nicknamed 'cocky locks.' Her daughter Caroline, born in 1907, believes that although her father was a master carpenter, their standard of living was helped by the fact that he also worked in the evenings in the box office of the Grand Theatre, Swansea. Another sign of affluence was the fact that their father was able to buy his five children season tickets to ride the Mumbles Train:

> These tickets entitled us to ride on what was called the Sandwich Train. This was the middle coach of three. The one on each end had wooden seats, but the Sandwich Train had much more comfortable seats.

Mary Thomas left school at fourteen in 1933. Her first job was in a ladies and children's outfitters. But when she was sixteen her parents decided to have her apprenticed to a qualified dressmaker. For the first two years she received no wages at all. When she left five years later she was earning £1 a week at the age of twenty-one. Her parents probably thought they had done the very best for her: she had a trade and could use her expertise when she got married. Other girls were not so lucky. Mary remembers that:

Many girls worked at various tin works in the Briton Ferry area. Their job was separating the tin sheets after they had cooled down. The job was dangerous, and very arduous, the hours were long and the wages were poor.

Some girls went as shop assistants, mostly in small shops. They worked long hours, too, six days a week. Wages were very poor, something like 7s.6d. a week.

The other alternative was to go into domestic service. This meant leaving home to go to London. Professional people in London, probably Welsh themselves, preferred young Welsh girls, and would advertise in the local papers for these girls. They would advertise the jobs in a very attractive way so that there were lots of applicants. Most of the situations were, in fact, far from attractive. The girls soon realized that they were trapped into drudgery. They were at the beck and call of the cook and housekeeper. Hours were long, with one half day off a week. Even on their half day off they had to be back in time to clear up after supper. Wages were a pittance. Things were not much better for the boys. For most, it was a job in the tin works, the steel works or as errand boys in small shops.

Very few boys or girls went on to higher education and academic careers.

Lena Harris, whose father was a colliery examiner in Abertillery, was lucky enough to go to grammar school. When she left in 1914 Lena went to work as a clerk in Lipton's: it was a seventy-three hour week. She had to be in the shop by 8.30.am. and Monday to Friday stayed until 8.pm. But on Saturday the shop stayed open until midnight when her father came to collect her in order to make sure she got home safely.

Ellen May Roberts was determined to become a nurse. Her father was a colliery fireman with five children and probably earned around £2.10s.0d. a week. They lived quite well on this wage, and her mother even took holidays away from home, going to her parents in Llangollen while a 'girl' was paid to look after the children while she was away. Ellen believes that her grandmother 'helped' the family, and she certainly paid for her books when she was training to become a nurse.

35

When she left school at fourteen, Ellen went to work in a wallpaper shop, but this was only a temporary job until she was seventeen and could start her training: she went as a trainee nurse to the tuberculosis hospital, Glan Ely, in Cardiff.

Another girl who wanted to be a nurse, was Edna Perry. Her father was unemployed in 1926, and so her mother received 2s. a week towards her keep. As soon as she left school this was stopped. At fourteen she went to the Mirror Laundry in Port Talbot and worked at a steam press. Edna worked a thirty hour week for 6s. She managed to get through the tedious pressing of bed linen because she knew it was a temporary job until she was old enough "to take up nursing." In September 1927 when she was nearly sixteen, she was sent to The National Hospital, East Finchley in London, to become the matron's maid:

> It was actually the convalescent home of The National Hospital for Nervous Diseases, Queen's Square, Bloomsbury, and in the style of a country house. Matron was Anglo-Indian, a kind, caring person. I became her maid because my main ambition was to be a nurse, but at my age I was too young. Also, my father wanted to be sure that I would be able to complete my training when I became eligible, because a contract would have to be signed and were I to break that contract by leaving (misconduct or marrying) a fee would have to be paid. This my parents would not be able to do.
>
> During my time as matron's maid she gave me an insight into what a nurse's training would be like: allowing me to serve food to female patients, some bed-ridden. I served some male patients who were "up and dressed", not in bed "because of my age."
>
> My pay was £1.10s.0d. a month and £1 was sent to my parents because at this time my father was, like many thousands of others, out of work. Annual holidays was a fortnight a year, for which I gave matron 2s.6d. a month to save for my train fare. Whilst looking back to my days at East Finchley it seems to have been an easy post, but for a 15½ to 17½ year-old away from home, it was very hard. Making sure I served matron's meals on nicely laid trays and accepting strict, but kind, discipline, became a way of life. Just a few months before my eighteenth birthday I returned to Port Talbot. The main reason matron advised me to return to Port Talbot to apply for a nursing career was that it was deemed to be "infra dig" to progress from a maid to nurse.

Brenda Hood's mother had found her work when she was fourteen, as soon as she left school in Pontarddulais:

My mother had got me a post as a children's nurse to two children: a girl of twenty-six months and a little boy of eight months. The master was lovely, but *she* was a madam. It was in a big house. The mistress was Polish and they went to Poland so that she could visit her parents there. At that time Hitler was on the scene and he was invading Poland and so she perhaps wouldn't see her parents alive. I was there just six weeks, but I was treated wonderfully. But I had to do all the children's washing by hand, the nappies in cold water: lucky it was summer. I received 5s. per week and my food.

When I left there I went to work for Gwilym Jones of Goppa Row. I was there for eight months. 5s. per week again, living-in—not bad—but very hard work because Sarah his wife was a sick woman and in bed for most of the time. Up at six and not in bed until 10 o'clock at night: with all the washing, ironing, cooking and baking to do. One afternoon a week off and every other Sunday. I liked my chapel, but wasn't able to go—only every other week—anyway I felt that I was being worked too hard: so I left, still friends and got a job in Clayton Tinplate Works. Great fun. 11s. a week 6 till 2 and Saturday morning 6 till 11. We were paid every two weeks, but it was steady hours, even if we *were* tired on finishing.

I worked in the Tin House, standing all day at a bench. The tin sheets would be pushed through the bran to get the grease off them. One girl would pick up a sheet and put it in the bran. Then they got passed to me and I had to dust off the bran before they were put in the rack. It was really hard work for a fourteen-year-old. They gave me a sheepskin apron and mitts to wear to protect my hands. Girls would go home totally exhausted. Most of the sheets went off to Nestle's Milk factory.

Lettice Maud Argust born in 1912 had a father who was a collier in Treherbert, supporting nine children on £1.10s.0d. a week. When Lettice left school in 1926 she went into service, first of all as a housemaid. She did not live-in, and worked from 9am. 'til 6pm. for 4s.6d. a week, which she gave to her mother. Lettice remembers eating better food in domestic service as she was given the "left-overs from the dining-room." When she was fifteen she joined the Girls Friendly Society which helped her to find employment in London. Lettice went from a close-knit community, where neighbours would push a piano out into the street of a Sunday afternoon and gather to sing together, to a huge metropolis. In Treherbert her life had revolved around the chapel. She saw her grandparents daily, and other relatives frequently. At fifteen all this changed; Lettice sometimes cried as she recalled her time in London:

The Girl's Friendly Society did not pay my fare to London, nor help with my uniform. I was instructed to wait at Paddington station with a flower in my coat, until I was collected. My new employer was the landlady of an upper-class residential boarding house in Notting Hill Gate. I was to be the kitchen maid at 7s.6d. a week, with a half day off in the week and every other Sunday.

My hours were 6 30.am. 'til 10pm. A long day. The first job of the day was to light all the fires throughout the house; clean the front and scrub the step: then polish all the brass on the door. Then it was time to help cook prepare the breakfast: serving it was exhausting as some were in the dining-room and some up four flights of stairs in bed. It was worse than being a housemaid previously. Whenever I had some spare money it was sent home to my mother. Once I saved up £3 but sent it all home so that my siblings could go on chapel outings. The rest of the staff there were bossy: all of them.

The family always gave orders politely, in a charming manner: but there was no real contact with them, not as a kitchen maid. The food was worse than in Wales. Nothing nice. On my half day off I would go and see my sister who was also in service in London, at Marble Arch: we just stayed in the basement talking. At least every other Sunday my sister arranged the same day off and we would go to walk in the park. For me London was overpowering. Too busy. Too big. And I was very homesick. I got to the stage where I couldn't even look at myself in the mirror without crying. I continually cried when I went to see my sister. My employers forbade me to use the telephone to ring her.

Eventually my mother came up to London to bring me home: but the homesickness left as soon as I saw her face. From that time I felt better, and stopped writing these tear-stained letters home. I decided to stay on, advancing from general housemaid to cook at 10s. a week. One job I left in London (with a clergyman) was because the vicar kept trying to trap me in the linen room. I didn't really understand what he wanted, but felt it was *wrong:* so I gave in my notice.

One of my sisters, Margaret, three years older than me, worked for a Jewish family: we all agreed they were the best employers. When I got to be eighteen I decided that I was ready to go back to South Wales and found a job as cook-housekeeper to a doctor and his wife at 10s.6d.

My life was one of unfulfilled dreams: to be a dressmaker and to learn to play the piano.

Another young exile, Sarah Bowen, who left Merthyr Tydfil when she was sixteen in 1933 to be a nanny in Bayswater, also felt terribly homesick and "many times" walked through Paddington Station "in the hope of seeing a face" she knew. When she recognised a policeman on point duty at Marble Arch, Bryn Philips from Twynylodyn, she was "quite overcome".

The 1920s and 30s saw the great *diaspora* of Welsh families as they left Wales for jobs elsewhere. Rhys Thomas growing up in Ammanford recalls: "it was tragic that the depression was such that hundreds of families up and left mainly to Midland Pits, to Birmingham, Wolverhampton, and of course, London. Friends disappeared almost overnight—and their memory died with their departure." In some families, only the children left home. Girls as young as fourteen or fifteen were sent away to work in England where there were jobs available—especially as domestic servants. But even a girl who had attended secretarial college could not always find work in Wales. Mabel Grenfell who was sixteen in 1928 bitterly resented all her life the fact that she had been sent away by her parents to live with cousins in London in order to search for work:

> The unemployment was so rife and at that time I could not get a job— neither could Pa—Alys and I were over the age for maintenance. Somehow I knew that Ma could not keep us both[2]. So she arranged for me to go "like a lamb to the slaughter". And why me? I was trained commercially.
>
> It was bewildering: going away like that. The only advice I had was from my Sunday School teacher—which I did not understand at the time: but it stayed with me. Ma arranged for me to go first of all to her cousin Will. The least said about those days the better. I was a qualified typist and soon found a job at the Head Office of the Port of London Authority. Of course, being there, the accommodation was good. I do not remember the rate of pay. I had to make it do, anyway. I felt that I had lost out on the arrangement and that Alys had the best deal. From then on I only went home twice a year: at Christmas and for my annual holiday.
>
> I cannot write anymore. I am filled with grief.

---

[2] Mabel was the elder of twin girls born in 1912.

But Mabel was fortunate that her parents had seen that she had a profession: her work hours were better, her rate of pay higher and she had more independence than those girls who were servants.

More fortunate girls with a father who could afford to send them to college had much wider horizons than those girls who entered domestic service or the local tin plate works. Bessie Higgs, born in 1911, the daughter of John Higgs the schoolmaster of Tirdeunaw Elementary School, north of Swansea, had a parent who expected her to have a profession. Bessie's mother had been trained as a teacher, and so it must have seemed natural that she would follow in her mother's footsteps. It was decided to send her to University College, Swansea. In 1930 when she was approaching twenty, she was sent to Aberdare Hall, the hostel for girls going to University College, Cardiff. Bessie had changed colleges in order to study botany, zoology and geology as one could not take sciences at Swansea. An incident which Bessie recalls at Aberdare Hall illustrates the power young women could exert when they took concerted action against a regime they did not like:

> Going to the hostel we had to supply our own bed linen and towels. My trunk hadn't arrived, and so the warden, Miss Katie Hurlbatt was very annoyed with me. She was tall, stern and already 82 years of age. All the girls were asked upon admission if they were constipated. It was an obsession. She told us all to get an orange a day, squeeze out the juice, add raisins, and take it. *That* would keep us *regular*.
> We girls resented Miss Hurlbatt. She was old, and very, very strict. And so we organised a *riot* against her strict discipline. It was well organised. It started on one floor, and then went on at each floor in turn and mounting in noise. We hurled bin lids down the corridors and made a dreadful commotion. We used anything which made a noise, and shouted our heads off. It was an awful *din*. It was after lights out at 10 o'clock. There was *pandemonium*. All the girls participated, about seventy of us. Miss Hurlbatt could do nothing. She was powerless.
> Soon after this riot she left and Miss Parry, a much younger woman was appointed warden. Tall, good-looking, about forty to fifty, very nice, always beautifully dressed and well connected. The atmosphere at Aberdare Hall changed. We could now entertain our men friends in the library. There was a dance every Christmas. The girls in the hall decorated the place for these

dances and made lemonade (lemons and citric acid), that was all we were allowed to drink. There would be a band.

The organised riot described here offers an alternative image from the stereotypical passive female who accepts authority. During the inter-war period young women were becoming more boisterous in their attempts to break free of the earlier constraints. Bessie became a teacher, but there were other professions open to girls. Megan Jones, born in 1915, the daughter of William Jones of Pencoed went to the Welsh College of Pharmacy—to Apothecary Hall—in Cardiff to train as a dispenser. After her training Megan went to work in a chemist's shop, but when war broke out in 1939 she found out that there was much more money to be earned at the Ordnance Factory in Bridgend:

> I wasn't going to stay in that chemist shop for 35s. a week. So off I went to become a clerical assistant, first class, at the Ordnance Factory. Oh! We had the time of our life.

The choice of jobs for most was severely limited. Boys left school to go into the mines or local steel works where the work was exhausting. But some parents were determined to give their children a much better chance in life than they themselves had had. Phyllis Llewellyn's father was a colliery check weigher in Porth with nine children. Phyllis, the eighth child was born in 1915: "out of the nine children, seven received a grammar school education and all four boys got apprenticeships." One girl went to university and Phyllis, despite her father having died when she was thirteen, trained as a nurse. Her parents Thomas and Rachel Llewellyn must have made many sacrifices in order to give their children such opportunities. Joseph Henry Fullard, born in Pontnewynydd, Pontypool was the second child of an English couple attracted to south Wales some time before his birth in 1912. His father had been born in Wolverhampton, the son of a bell founder and brass finisher, and migrated to Pontypool where he found work in the steel works. His mother was a Londoner, from Golders Green, the daughter of a cooper. They were to have eight children. Joseph left school on his fourteenth birthday: September 27th 1926:

There was a strike on when I left school with the miners and steel workers out. When the strike was over I was able to start working at Pontnewynydd Steel and Sheet Works: for five days I worked from 6am. to 4.pm., but on Saturdays it was 6.am. to 12 noon. The wages were 15s. out of which I paid a penny for the doctor and a penny for the hospital each week. When I got home I gave my wage packet to my mother who then gave me half-a-crown back as my pocket money.

There was no choice of other employment: you were either a steel-worker or a collier. That was it. The clothes I wore to work consisted of an old pair of trousers, a grey Welsh flannel shirt (short sleeves), a sweat towel, which I wore around my neck to wipe away the sweat running into my eyes. At the end of the shift my shirt was stiff and white with salt. I also wore clogs which were most comfortable. The steel tips on the clogs stopped them burning away by the hot steel plates we worked on. In the summer the heat was almost unbearable: the furnace at the back of you, hot rolls in front of you—through which we put the red hot steel, rolling it into various lengths.

John Thomas Protheroe left Ynyswen School when he was thirteen in 1912 and first of all had a job in the lamproom at the local colliery, working a twelve hour shift. When he reached fourteen he was able to go down to the coal face and started working nights: 10pm. to 7am. He earned "half a gold sovereign a week." Paid in gold, he would give the half sovereign to his mother who then gave him 6d. pocket-money back. When war broke out he was only fifteen and in a reserved occupation; but in 1918 when he was eighteen he decided to join the Royal Welch Fusiliers and with the 14th Battalion went to fight in France.

John James Jones, born in 1895, the son of James Jones, was brought up in Manselton, Swansea. The family house on Phillip Street was close to Cwmfelin Works where his father worked as a tin-plate worker. When he left Manselton Boys School in 1908 he was thirteen years old:

I had been in the top class for two years and then when the August holidays were nearly over a neighbour told me that there was a vacancy for a boy at the Cambria Daily Leader office in Castle Bailey Street. On the Monday morning instead of going back to school I went and applied for the job and got it. Then I went up to school and spoke to the headmaster asking if I could leave as I had a job, and he said O.K. I started work after dinner that very day.

At the newspaper office I was employed as a copy boy. My wages were 5s. a week. It was enjoyable work. Part of my duties was to go to the Police Court at the Old Town Hall at the bottom of the town and get the report of the cases from the reporter and bring them back to the office. This job only lasted four months as I had to give it up owing to a bout of lead poisoning caused by lead fumes from the molten lead from the foundry at the press shop.

My next job was coffee roasting at The Kardomah in Castle Street. Around fourteen years old still. I had to get in by 8.30.am. and start coffee roasting. I also made deliveries. They gave me a handtruck with a tea-chest on it full of parcels. Some houses would just have a quarter of tea delivered. One day was set aside for deliveries in the Mumbles area. I would take the Mumbles train down around the bay (having been allowed to take my truck onto the train). Another day was set aside for deliveries in Morriston: then I'd take the tram up to Tabernacle.

When I was fifteen—at last—I achieved my ambition and became a tin-plate worker at Cwmfelin Works. My father did not like the idea at all, as he knew what a hard life it was. Anyway, I had my own way. And started work in what they called the cold rolling department. We all wore canvas aprons and leather pads made from old shoe-uppers to protect our hands. The standard size of tinplate was twenty-eight inches by twenty inches and we carried as many as we could down to the annealing plant. It was, indeed, very hard work. But at last, I thought, I'm a man.

And with 'manhood' one started to think of 'courting.' David Killa recalls what were called the "Bunny Runs" in pre-war Swansea.

Up until the wartime black-out, there were at least four areas of Swansea which had become the mecca of the youth of the town and the surrounding areas on Sunday evenings. Early in the evening, boys and girls would begin to converge on these areas and as chapel services ended there would be a rush to join the throng of youngsters who paraded up and down the 'bunny runs' of Caereithin, Oxford Street, The Promenade, and from Cwm Level Road to Cwmgelli cemetery. The aim was to walk up and down the road and try to make conversation with the ones you fancied. If you 'clicked', that is, had a smile or nod from the one you fancied, you would go off together, and get to know each other better. It was fun and more good came from it than bad.

The months or years of courting offered young people a brief spell of comparative freedom between school and marriage, between their own childhood and the years of parenthood that lay ahead. Young men could be a 'bit rebellious' without ruining a family's reputation, but young women had much narrower parameters. Lilian Jones[3] as a young working woman remembers:

> One Sunday I was down at Langland Bay with a group of friends, just sitting on the grass, talking. Just enjoying all the talk. It was blistering hot and so I'd taken off my silk stockings. My legs were all bare. And who should walk past out of the blue but my Dada with Mama too. I nearly died. It was shameful to be seen without your stockings on: common. I knew there would be a dreadful scene when I got home. And there was.

There was always a price to pay for breaking the rules. Girls especially had to be most circumspect in their behaviour. One's reputation still remained of paramount importance.

Once courting started their time would be spent walking, attending church services, going to the cinema when they had the money, visiting relatives and sitting together 'in the front parlour': a room central to a daughter's courtship ritual. In a family with a number of marriageable daughters occupation of the parlour had to be on a rota system once young women got down to the serious business of life: courting. They accepted that their acknowledged role was to be wife and mother.

With parenthood then as now, came the end of childhood. For many, responsibilities in the family and in the world outside had made them leave the years of childhood at a much younger age, as their stories will show.

I am grateful to all the respondents who shared with me memories of their lives. I am saddened that several who speak to you through the pages of this book have since died. Their stories, for us, breathe life into a time and place that we might not otherwise have known half as well.

[3] Her grandfather had made the pews in Sketty Church, Swansea, when the Vivians were having it built. The family were wealthy industrialists and lived at Singleton Abbey. When the Vivians asked for a suitable boy to be found at Sketty School to go and play at the Abbey with Lord Swansea's children, it was Lilian's father who was chosen. Later he named his first girl after Lord Swansea's daughter: "and the family always stopped their carriage to talk to him when he grew up".

NELLIE LILIAN MURIEL HOWELL OF CARDIFF

Born November 13th, 1888
Daughter of George Bevan Howell, and his wife
Florence Mary Howell née Shelper.

I was the eldest child of a family of four girls who all survived childhood, and was born in a house on Orange Street near the Old Swansea Market.

When I was five or six we all went to live in Cardiff, where I first went to the Municipal School for a short time, but later transferred to St. Edmundsbury School in Willfield Road which was kept by a Mrs. Jennings and her two daughters. It was a nice school where we girls learned Algebra, English, History, Drawing and a little French. Lessons started at the convenient hour of 10 a.m. with a break for lunch and then more work until 3.30 p.m. to 4 p.m. I stayed with Mrs. Jennings until I was nearly seventeen, quite satisfied with the curriculum which was divided between the mother and her daughters: their main aim was to produce 'ladies'.

Our mother was strict but gentle in her ways. She always worried a great deal about our father when he was away at sea: he was a marine engineer. One year he returned from *Santos*, which was a very feverish place, and fell ill with Scarlet Fever, which one of my sisters also caught from him. Mother would go to meet our father at his first port of call and then Grandma Shelper would come to look after us.

We girls had to keep our bedrooms dusted and our 'things' tidy, but were never expected to help with the cleaning or cooking. There was a daily domestic to do the housework, but mother always did the cooking. The routine of our daily lives was not rigidly controlled, no set days for baths or washing hair. Mother was quiet and affectionate. Father was as strict as our mother, but kind and thoughtful; he was an avid reader and fond of dogs. I believe father was a 'lively spark' but saw to it that his daughters were 'ladylike.' He had been educated at St. Andrews School in Swansea and enjoyed telling us about a particular master there, whose daily routine upon entering a classroom was to poke the fire vigorously. One particular day a boy placed the handle to heat in the coals and just before the master entered, turned it round and put it in its usual position. How the boys laughed when the poor man picked up the poker and jumped with shock at finding the handle red-hot.

When we lived in Cardiff we used to look forward, very much, to Sunday morning, for we were then allowed to go out by ourselves to see if there was any mail to be collected from the Post Office, as there was no delivery. This was a weekly treat: it gave us a little freedom. After our walk we would have breakfast, then a passage would be read from the Bible and prayers in the dining-room. If we were in Bristol where Grandpa Shelper lived, he would read and say the prayers. After lunch we all went to Sunday School where Grandpa was Superintendent. (In Cardiff we went to Woodville Road Baptist Chapel.) After tea there would be prayers again at 8.30 p.m. and then straight to bed. Sometimes we would get Fry's Chocolate Cream as a treat when being tucked up in bed.

I remember when I was nine a very lively relation of my Aunt Rosie coming to stay; he was full of mischief and once gilded all the flowers in the conservatory. He was larking on the staircase one day whilst I was going up and kicked out my two front teeth. Of course, I cried alarmingly and to appease me the adults confessed that there was no Father Christmas. I was so pleased at being confided with this piece of information and thought myself rather superior at knowing he did not, in fact, exist.

At Christmas time our presents were wrapped and always put on the side plates on the breakfast table in the breakfast room. We never had a Christmas tree, just evergreens brought in from the garden, holly and cotoneaster with its bright red berries. There would be games of Blind Man's Buff.

There was no such thing as physical punishment when I was a child; we would feel admonished just by a frown from either of our parents. I volunteered to go to Christian Endeavour and Band of Hope just to get out of the house, as there was no freedom of movement. We were strictly supervised, up to a point, and I desperately wanted to get out and about and see and do things. The only means of getting out to relieve the monotony of home life were those activities offered by

Christian Endeavour and Band of Hope. I didn't particularly want to get involved with these religious groups, but it presented an avenue of escape and would gain the wholehearted approval of my parents. Even then I was only allowed to attend because a spinster aunt consented to take me. Supervision was all important for girls.

We learned painting naturally, but dancing lessons were unheard of, if they had been suggested our father would probably have forbidden them, we just didn't think of such things. We had *Chatterbox* and *Girls Own* to read. Every girl read *Jessica's First Prayer*, it was a *must*, and I remember shedding copious tears over the story.

Our holidays were always divided between the Grandparents in Swansea and Bristol. Great Grandpa Shelper had built a substantial detached house called *Sunnybanke* at Down End in Bristol. There the daily routine was quite rigid and never changed. We would breakfast at 8.30 a.m., then have coffee at 11 a.m. with lunch served promptly at 1 p.m; afternoon tea would be served at 3.30 p.m. followed by high-tea at 5.30 p.m. Great Grandpa Shelper was a builder and kept a resident maid. There was a lot of garden which the boys from the Sunday School would help maintain. There was a kitchen garden, an orchard and a pond with water-cress. I remember that the kitchen there was flag-stoned with a pump connected to a well; there were no taps in the house at all.

Grandpa Howell lived above his Wholesale and Retail business on Orchard Street in Swansea. Behind the premises there was quite a lot of stabling which he needed, and visitors to the town from the country were allowed to rest there and eat their provisions. He kept his own saddle horse as well as an assortment of carts and a gig. In the shop there were always great mounds of butter; if customers wished to taste a sample they would take out a silver bit from their pocket and nick a bit off. That seemed to be the customary practice: it gave them a taste before they bought it. Not very hygienic.

Our lives changed when my mother died at thirty-nine years of age in 1906; I was just eighteen and with my three sisters was brought to Swansea to live with Grandma Howell. At the time I was determined to go out to work, which upset my grandmother considerably. She was convinced that such a step would see me firmly on the road to Hell.

We had not been brought up to think of jobs for ourselves. When grandmother realised that I was determined, she decided that a job in Ben Evans the departmental store would be the most suitable occupation. But to her horror I embarked on a shorthand and typing course and got a job in a Shipping Office. That was a considerable achievement in those days. Girls usually did as they were told, and certainly our grandparents would have preferred us to stay at home. For me it was like breaking free.

SAMUEL EDMUNDS OF PENRHIW-FER, RHONDDA

Born December 11th, 1894
Son of John Edmunds and his wife
Jane Edmunds, née Evans.

My father, who was an underground haulier at the pit, was born in Maesteg. He and his parents moved to Penrhiw-fer near Pen-y-graig in the Rhondda looking for work, because a new pit opened there. Mother's family came from Llanidloes where they kept a pub, they came down looking for work, too.

I was born in Glamorgan Terrace, number thirty, in Penrhiw-fer, the only child; they never explained why I was the only one, I was never told. It was quite unusual in those days, there were always more in families. Mrs. Reynolds, the midwife, delivered me, she went to whoever required one.

At four I went to Penrhiw-fer Infants. We had chalk on boards, and a bit of reading and writing. At the big school, which was Williamstown Boys School, the master was strict, he was the boss. Kind he was, but you had to do what you were told, he had control. The atmosphere was good, I'd say, the masters had a cane, but they wouldn't use it just for the sake of it. You'd have to do something wrong. If you flicked paper around, or chewed anything, like sweets, that would get you caned. Mind, if you had the cane you wouldn't go home and say you'd had a crack from the teachers, 'cos your father would give you another. And if my father said no, that was it. He was the boss of me. I didn't like school, there didn't seem anything in it for me. The future was underground, no matter who your friends were, it was the colliery, very few of our friends went into shops.

They didn't make me do jobs at home, but I'd do the brass on a Friday night to pass an hour. We had a bit of brass. Mother had a washing day, she'd do that all day. She had a tub, the clothes had to be boiled in a copper on the fire. The water had to be brought in in jacks for drinking, we went up to what we called the spout, off the road, it was a spring, lovely mountain water, beautiful, it was a treat, just about one hundred yards from the house. A jack isn't like a bucket, it's narrow and made of metal. For washing there was a cask of water under the shute, that was soft rainwater for all our washing. Mam had to do all her washing scrubbing away at the scrubbing board, it would all be dollied to get it clean. In the kitchen it was all stone floors, they had to be scrubbed. There was a bit of oil-cloth on the floor until we could afford a bit of mat. We had three bedrooms, two were big, you could get several beds in them, so we weren't overcrowded. It was all right having a bedroom of my own. My mother looked after the house. Dad wouldn't help, he started work at 7 a.m. until 5 p.m. In the winter he wouldn't see any daylight.

Dad had his hand off, left hand, in the mines with the tram. He was a haulier and lost his hand. There was no compensation as such in those days, but he did get twenty-five pounds for the loss of his hand. He was brought home. I was in the house at the time, this was around 1901. They took him to hospital to have it off. As he couldn't go back down the pit at that time, he bought two horses and a brake and after getting a licence from the Council he started as a brake-driver, out all day collecting people from the train station. Take them home he would, Dinas Station to Pen-y-graig. Then he'd take boozers home from the pubs. Fridays, Saturdays, he always got paid, he always got his fare even if they were laugh-drunk. When the trams came about 1910, his business was done away with. He had to go back to the mine. They gave him a light job underground.

As Dad only had one hand it was my job to look after the garden. It was a two-fronted garden. I grew all our veg, mostly spuds, but some carrots and cabbage, plenty of mint. I had to do this from a young age. There'd be some advice from the old gardeners around. We paid a farmer about five bob a year to keep chickens, open-range like, down in his field. There was a cot there, too, where Dad kept his horses and brake. When he gave that up, the farmer allowed him to keep the chickens there, he loved keeping chickens and we had ducks, too, as there was a pond. It was a sloping field so you couldn't play games. And you didn't have to carry water down as there was plenty there.

I went home for dinner. There'd be all kinds of meat, and we had our own chickens so if we fancied that we'd have one. Then there might be chops, or sausages. When I went as a grocer's boy at the age of twelve I had two shillings a week. I went every afternoon straight from school at twelve o'clock. He had all my deliveries ready and I did them on my way home for my dinner. Some nights, usually on a Thursday, I went straight after tea to help take faggots to the bakers, wait for them to be done, well, hang about anyway, then take them back to the shop. They'd be ready for Friday, 'cos Friday was a big faggot day, with peas. I'd have to call in on a Friday, but Saturday was my big day. I went to work at eight o'clock, first to clean windows, ready for eight-thirty, then inside to serve butter, weigh potatoes. He'd give me my dinner on a Saturday, sausages usually, that was cheap, then work until midnight. The town at nine-thirty or ten was crowded with people. Men got paid on a Saturday, so women had to wait for their money. The men went home with their money, they'd bath and clean up then go out for beer and the women to the shops 'til half the night. It was a long day for me at twelve. At midnight the butcher would give me a bit of meat, a few chops, so that would help out at home, and I got two shillings. Nothing from the grocer, they were tight then, the grocer and the butcher were the same family see. Mam had the two shillings and I had enough to go to the pictures, threepence in the Gods, then fish and chips for tuppence, and a bottle of pop for a penny, sixpence worth, that was my evening out.

Dad never touched me, if he said no, it was no good carrying on, no was no. He never beat me, not what you'd call a hiding. Some parents were strict, boys did get a beating, and kept indoors. My parents never argued, not what you'd call a row, they were affectionate. Mind, he'd do what he wanted to do, and she'd do what she wanted. In the winter we'd have a game of dominoes together, sometimes cards, though Dad was better at handling dominoes.

The Sunday School outing to Barry Island was the big treat, we'd all wait for that, and also the choir would have a brake outing to Porthcawl on Whit Monday or Easter Monday. It was by train to Barry, as the men couldn't go on a weekday, they changed it to a Saturday, so then the men could go if they wanted. May Day was a big day in Penrhiw-fer with open air meetings. It was a day off from work, one out of the twelve you were allowed, without pay mind. No pay, you'd have two days Easter, then May Day, three at Whitsun, three in August and three at Christmas, that's your twelve days holiday allowed yearly. On May Day there'd be a procession, then Labour MPs speaking to the assembled men. And the chapels would have a very big day. Those that went a distance would take sandwiches. My Dad didn't go to these May Day meetings.

Our house was rented, my cousin owned it. We could have lived there for ever at seven shillings and sixpence a week. We moved only once, from one street to another, to Caemawr Terrace, number ten, but later on, back again to twenty-nine Glamorgan Terrace as my mother thought it a better place, it had a good view, there was no houses in front of you. All open fields. The cousins owned twenty-nine and thirty.

My Dad earned about one pound fifteen shillings down the mine. Mind, the collier didn't get a wage, only what he cut, and had to pay his boy out of that according to his age. Dad did only light jobs 'cos of his hand, helping to put dust alongside the roads underground to stop explosions, that sort of thing. Dad died young after. They said it was asthma then, but now they know it's silicosis. He was fifty-seven, that's all. Mind you, if you were sixty in those days you were considered an old man.

We had comic books, *Titbits* weekly. At Sunday School they gave us a Bible to read, then collected them in. If they gave prizes for attendance, it was a Bible, no other book. Dad read *The Weekly Despatch* on a Sunday, and the *Empire News*, both on Sunday; Mam and Dad shared, they exchanged papers when they'd finished. Then they had the daily *Western Mail*.

We didn't have a proper playing field. There was a bit of ground near the houses and we'd make that do. Make the best of it, and we had a bit of an ash-tip, all flat, there we'd play Cati. You had a handle, that was the dog, then the cati which was a stick like, both sharpened, and you hit the point of the cati with the dog for it to jump. Then you tried to hit it as it came up, and hit it as far as you could back to the dab, that's the place where you started. Then you measured with the dog the distance it was from the dab. That was how you scored. There was marbles, too, that was a big game. We didn't hardly mix with girls, they wouldn't play Cati, that's cat and dog, they'd play scotch on the markers, whip and top.

If we had a football, it was made out of rags or papers, until that policeman came. We'd play, then when he'd arrive you'd be off. The policeman was good mind. If we trespassed, or played football on the road, he wouldn't summons us because he said it was the parents who'd have to pay, not us. But if he caught us he'd give us a good hiding, we'd not forget it. He'd say that gave us a lesson, it was better than a summons. That policeman knew us all, he could get us if he wanted to, he only had to go to the house. If he had hold of you he would bother, a good beating we had, but he never bore a grudge after it was all over.

We boys went in for a lot of knocking on doors, tying handles together first. We'd tie two front door handles together, see, they were terraced houses, then we'd nip round the back, or another two would go round the back and tie the back doors together. Then we'd knock on the front doors and they couldn't open them. They'd have to get the next-door but one to get the rope off. We'd be gone. We'd know which way to go. And there was buckets of water tipped up against the back door, not the front door, 'cos there was a tub at the back door, the water was easy to get and there'd be a bucket back there, too. We'd knock hard, they'd come to the door, and the water would tip in. You'd make sure that bucket tipped into the house.

A good place to keep things, like cotton reels, and bottles of ink, was the window frame, you know, the middle part. You could get a hat-pin, shove it up between the two windows and knock everything off, over they'd go. We were never caught. There were only windows at the front of the houses, and a window at the top of the stairs, no windows at the back. All the lavs were outside. Another trick we had, we tied the back door to the bucket in the lav, and when they opened the door the bucket overturned all down the back-yard. We had to go after that, up the backfield out of the way. It wasn't fun to them, but it was fun for us. We'd have made foot-holes in the wall that led up to the field, for a quick getaway. We had it all planned. We liked a game of rounders on this bit of ground, the policeman would come and watch us, we played a lot of that in the summer. There was no such thing as hobbies.

There was Band-of-Hope, somewhere for us to go I suppose. They were interesting evenings, of course. Oh! We'd have an hour or an hour and a half. They'd have people in to entertain us, comics to tell yarns, singers, there'd be recitations. For fund raising the Church would hold a Cantata before Lent, you didn't do much in Lent. They used to have a pancake tea on the Tuesday before Ash Wednesday. On a Sunday there was Church at eleven o'clock, Sunday school at two-thirty and evening service at six. I was in the choir, every year we had a choir outing in horse and brakes. There was no choir pay, so if you'd had enough you could come out of it. We'd enjoy Sunday, we met everyone.

If you went to Church they always thought you was a Tory. If you went to the Baptists you were Liberal. Labour was hardly out then. Dad wasn't a Tory, he went to Church but was Liberal, that's what he voted until Labour came more into power. My parents expected me to go to Church while I was in school. But when I started work at fourteen they let me have a kip on Sunday morning. They'd leave me in bed, but I went to Sunday school in the afternoon.

The doctor would come at once if we were ill, if it was urgent he'd even leave the surgery to his assistant, and come at once, he was good. Dad would pay at work weekly, so if the doctor was needed he'd come with no charge. My Mam didn't make any medicines. Mind, we'd pick tons of blackberries, make blackberry wine and jam. We grew a lot of rhubarb, that made good wine. We had an old Jew, a glazier, he'd put glass back in windows, from Russia he was, summer and winter he'd have an overcoat on. He'd come along and say, 'Give me a bit of that rhubarb.' You'd break a bit off and he'd eat it raw, just there, and enjoy it. I don't know how he could eat it raw. But he enjoyed it, and his hands all full of putty, too.

We always had a dark, best suit. It was put away on a Monday, never used in the week. After Church on Sundays it'd be brushed down, well that suit was always dark, and could be used for mourning if anyone died. You always had your best suit with a black tie. There was a lot of fuss then when anyone died. The third Sunday after burial there was always a memorial service, that'd give them time to get over the funeral, that used to be terrible, the hymns were terrible. Terrible hymns we'd sing:

Days and moments quickly flying
Blend the living with the dead.
Soon will you and I be lying
Each within our narrow bed.

Dear, they were mournful, with all the mourners crying. That's what it was like.

Well, at school the Labour Exam was set for December and I passed that. I stayed on the extra two weeks because I wanted my Christmas presents from school, what they were giving away for nothing. I wanted to be part of that. The teacher used to apply to firms for presents, games you know, puzzles like. We'd get Ludo, or Snakes and Ladders. Left school at fourteen, after Christmas, then I went on a regular basis to the grocer's and butcher's where I'd been working after school since I was ten. The butcher advertised the cinema programme in his window, and got a free pass. Well, he wouldn't go, so he'd give me the pass, and I'd go down to Tonypandy. Go on a Thursday night after school when the shop was closed. He wouldn't want me, he closed the shop and being a single chap he went dancing and I got the pass.

Now after Christmas I left school and went on a regular basis to the shop for three shillings and sixpence a week, it stayed open until twelve-thirty each Saturday night. I stayed there about six weeks at most as I was waiting for a job underground at the Ely pit in Pen-y-graig. At fourteen, there I was underground. The shift started at seven so I had to be out of the house at six-fifteen, then about a mile to walk. Down in the cage I'd go, then perhaps the best part of a mile down, underground to walk, always half a mile anyway.

I started off as a door-boy. They had to have doors every so often, to stop the air from building up in one place, and driving along. The doors were kept closed to break it up. You'd sit alongside that door, you'd make a bit of a seat with an old plank and a few bricks, there wasn't a proper seat made for you. You'd wait for the haulier with his tram and horse to come, and I'd have to open the door for him and shut it tight as soon as he'd gone through. Every quarter of an hour easy, I'd be opening the door, in and out the haulier would be. He'd go up with an empty tram, and come back with a full one from the face. For about six months I opened doors for two bob a day, six days a week, so I got twelve shillings at the end of it. That was fair considering the job, that wasn't hard work. There was only my oil lamp there beside the door, other than that, darkness. There were mice galore down there, plenty of mice. They couldn't get at my food because I had it in a Tommy-box made of tin, a bit of tin, so that was safe. They couldn't get at your grub. But if you had an apple in your pocket, they'd be in there, you'd find it all eaten, well, you couldn't eat it then. So I'd take an orange, they couldn't get much of that orange, what with the thick skin, so I'd have that, mind, my hands weren't very clean. If you took an apple down there you'd have to eat it straight away. You couldn't do much about those mice. We didn't take any notice of them. We didn't have rats.

After six months a chap asked me to be his collier-boy. That paid more, an extra sixpence a day, that's half-a-crown. Then, of course, as you got older you'd get extra coppers. As a collier-boy I helped to fill the tram, put coal in the tram. In time he'd show you how to use the hatchet, and the mandrel, or the pick if you know it by that name. If you had a good man, he'd show you, and after, if he'd earned good wages, that's over the minimum wage, he'd give you a tip. That was all to yourself, your Mam didn't know about tips, so you could spend it on yourself. Mam'd give me pocket money, five shillings, but with my tips I got more, but she didn't know. Mind, my Mam wouldn't crop me of it, she might have wanted me to save it. I'd buy sweets, or go to the pictures. I didn't have that pass then, I had to pay for my own pictures. We'd go every week, the usual was Saturday night.

You had to have so many years experience before you could go on your own underground, twenty or twenty-one before you could have a place. You weren't a proper collier until then. So I was six years or so, before I got my place. It was a sort of apprenticeship, that's what it was. I didn't expect any more. There was only the Corona factory, pop factory at Porth, and how often did they have a job going there? You'd have to wait for somebody to die. Then there were the shops, but not many jobs there, they'd employ relatives. It was underground for most of us. The girls went out to service, London, wherever they could get a place. They couldn't afford to keep them at home. After I'd started work the eight hour day came in. We had a terrible accident at the Ely pit, 1908 or 1909 it was. The carriage coming up the pit hit the sheave that the rope was around, and went back down the pit, and hit the cage that was already down there. Many men were killed, eight at least, because I went to three or four funerals. It was a terrible thing to happen.

FLORENCE AMOR OF CARDIFF

Born November 21st, 1897
Daughter of Frederick Amor and his wife
Louisa Amor née Small

My father, who was a railway clerk with the Great Western Railway, was born in Calne in Wiltshire, the son of a shoemaker. But my mother had been born in Westminster, London and had worked for a photographer before her marriage: 'touching up' photographs. Our Welsh connection came through my mother's mother who had been born in Carmarthenshire. There is quite a story. My maternal grandfather appeared to have had a very prosperous dairy business in London, and his milk came up from Wales, from Welsh farms: that's how he met my grandmother. The family prospects seem to have been very promising, as my mother and two sisters were sent to boarding school in Scarborough, and received a Lady's education, including music and art. When my mother was in her late teens the business seems to have collapsed and the family came to Cardiff. Later they appear in Mountain Ash where my mother's sister married, then again to Cardiff where my aunt's husband had a fruit and vegetable business. In the late 1870s when the family was in straightened circumstances, my aunt took several of her siblings to live with her, and my mother (who was something of an artist: having been taught painting and drawing at her boarding school) got a job with a photographer. It must have been difficult living with her sister, who doubtless was anxious to get the family off her hands as soon as possible. My mother always said she was *forced* into marriage. They were married at St. Margaret's Church, Rumney in 1879. It was not a love match.[1] She was twenty-three.

My mother was only eighteen when her father's business failed and the family split up. Parents had much more influence over their children than in these modern times and daughters who were dependent on their fathers had to be guided by them as to the suitability of prospective husbands. My mother always said that her

[1] By this time my grandparents had acquired Alva Farm, St. George's, on the Tredegar Estate.

elder sister forced her to marry my father, to get her off her hands. I cannot imagine that my parents wrote any love letters, as they were completely incompatible. I suppose she was considered lucky to get an offer of marriage, but she was so disillusioned that she was determined that her six daughters should be able to choose.

Our mother did not want a large family, partly because she was not very fond of children, and also for financial reasons. She was very ambitious and my parents had a very small income. She *begged* my father to limit the family to four children, but to no avail. We lived in rented houses: very few people owned their own houses and landlords were very reluctant to do repairs and so we moved frequently; seven times in twenty years.

I always knew that I was an unwanted child, the eighth of nine—but once my mother had them she worked her fingers to the bone to bring them up to her high standards and, most important, to help them to have a good education: she would have preferred all boys. However, she was to have seven girls and two sons who survived childbirth[2]. There were others, stillbirths, so she had more than nine pregnancies. One little girl died when she was only five weeks old and was buried in a public grave with others. After my own birth in 1897 I was shown to a great aunt who retorted, "Pity the Good Lord didn't take her," which illustrates the low status of girls in those days. The preference was for boys. Until 1914 it was a man's world. Boys were considered to have superior intellect: they had a wider curriculum at school and other advantages for advancement. However, having been landed with six daughters to bring up, our mother was determined that they should have the best education that was available at that time. She taught us to read and write and do simple arithmetic before we went to school. She encouraged us to work hard at our studies and later to take evening classes. She was most anxious for us to gain proper qualifications and to

[2] They were Lionel Valentine, born 1881, who became Chief Engineer at East Moors Works, Cardiff; Una Mildred, born 1883, she went to work in the Post Office; Olive Louise, born 1884, a domestic science mistress in a Hull school; Ida Dorothy, born 1886, who had no occupation and married in 1913; Muriel, born 1888, but died when she was only five weeks old; Elsie Vida, born in 1890, a mistress at Kesteven Girls' school, Grantham, and taught Mrs. Thatcher; Beatrice Ethel, born 1893, secretary; Florence Lillian, born 1897, who became a head teacher and Frederick Leslie, born in 1900.

aim at the professions that carried a pension, so that we could be completely independent. She *discouraged* us from marrying. Out of the six of us, only one did: that was Ida in 1913 when she was twenty-seven. I am afraid we girls took everything for granted and it was not until much later that we realised how many sacrifices she had made on our behalf.

Lately I have thought much about my father. I have decided that he was more sinned against than sinning. My parents were quite incompatible and had nothing in common, not even religion. When our father came from Calne to Cardiff he joined the Wesleyan Methodists and we were all brought up at Roath Road Church. My mother was an Anglican and did not take kindly to Methodism, but she always accompanied us. To all intents and purposes my father was a simple, uncomplicated, genial man, unambitious and content with his lot. He was always well dressed and well groomed, wore a starched white 'dicky' and cuffs, good quality shoes; a frock coat and silk hat on Sundays. I think that after the first three children were born, he opted out and left the management of the household entirely to my mother. As long as his clothes were ready and good, regular meals provided, he did not seem to take much part in the upbringing of the family. He had no interests and I never saw him read a book: apart from his job he was completely idle. No, I really did *not* know my father. He was supposed to have a very violent temper and strangely enough, I think that my mother was rather afraid of him. By the time I was born in 1897, there seems to have been a pattern and we knew that we must not upset our father. He could be very irritable.

When I was a child I was always conscious of my mother's general anxiety over managing such a large family and the costs involved. We had a lodger. And my elder sister Ida was kept at home once she finished school at fourteen, in order to help in the house. She then spent thirteen years as a general help until she got married and left home in her late twenties.[3] It was with my sister's help that my mother managed to run the household. She made all our clothes until we were earning our own money and then she encouraged us to buy classic

[3] After an engagement of several years Ida married the son of the Roath Road Methodist Church minister, the Reverend Bourne.

styles made of good material. When my uncle gave my mother a Wheeler and Wilson's treadle sewing machine it must have been a wonderful help and saved a lot of time. We girls had to make all our own underclothing and regularly mend and darn our woollen stockings. She set very high standards of dress. No frills or furbelows or make-up. Our mother did not have many clothes herself, but when she was dressed for going out, she looked very elegant. She was very particular about shoes, gloves and handkerchiefs. She wore tailored costumes, beautiful hand-made blouses with high necks—sometimes boned—and had a fur muff and feather boa. I was so proud of her and thought she would grace any social gathering.

Really, I do not know what my father earned, probably not more than a couple of pounds or so a week in the early 1900s to support ten of us. He was a clerk in the claims department of the railway. When goods were damaged in transit, firms refused to accept them and demanded compensation. My father dealt with the negotiations and if there was a court case, had to represent the railway. He was always very particular about his appearance.

The road in which we lived was known as 'Skipper's Alley' because so many sea-going captains and engineers lived there and they always seemed so affluent. By the time of the First World War, Cardiff had become a flourishing port and it was said that any man who worked at the docks could make a fortune. Certainly to own a ship was a plus. Our next door neighbour went to sea on a merchant ship: he came from Appledore in Devonshire, and had humble origins, but he became a captain. When he retired he invested in a ship, and later founded the City Line of merchant ships. He was given a knighthood, set up the Cardiff Nautical College and died a millionaire: he was Sir Reardon Smith.

My father was quite unimpressed by riches. He had a steady job which carried a pension. He had known intimately many of the Methodists who attended our fashionable church: they had often started lower down the social scale than he had. Some of them had very humble beginnings and were quite uneducated. In 1914 when the First World War came, they happened, by chance, to be in the right place, at the right time, and made fortunes. Cardiff docks was a hive of industry and world-wide shipping. We lived in old large Victorian terraced, rented houses, in a good neighbourhood and had five or six bedrooms. Most people with families lived in rented houses and it was not until after the War and wages improved, that home ownership was aspired to.

My mother, having been privately educated, did not like the Board Schools, so she sent my brother and older sisters to small Church schools, where the classes were small. However, we moved to another district where no Church schools were available, so some of my sisters had to attend the nearest Board School. It was big and cold. The classes were about fifty pupils. Discipline was more important than teaching. The Head Teacher harassed the teachers and they in their turn bullied and shouted at the children. My sisters hated it. The cane was often used. By the time I was six, another school had been built near our home and three of us attended it. The Head Teacher and staff were more humane and the discipline not so harsh. It was Marlborough Road School, Penylan, a council maintained school. As long as one *conformed* the teachers were kind. The outer school doors were always kept shut during lessons so that there was no parental access to individual teachers. As a rule the Head Teacher sat in the hall, not in a private room, and kept an eagle eye on everything and *everybody*.

As children we were lucky that our father worked for the Great Western, so we had 'privilege tickets' to travel: we could not have afforded to have gone otherwise. So we went on holidays: Burnham-on-Sea, Porthcawl, Ilfracombe, Penzance, Weston-Super-Mare (on the Paddle Steamer) and, of course, Barry. We played on the beach, bathed and watched the Punch and Judy shows. And there were Pierrots, too, playing on the sand. During the First World War we were able to take a furnished house at the seaside for the whole month of August. My mother must have been a wonderful financial manager, to feed, clothe and educate us so that we could be independent. Granted that commodities were relatively cheap and we could get scholarships for school and college, it must have been an ambitious task. By the time that I was born, the older members of the family were earning and could contribute to the family budget. During the war years we could afford to take a house for a month at the seaside.

My father and other members of the family came for part of the time and we would take excursions to places of interest. On Sundays we would always go to the services in little country churches. It was all very simple and unexciting, but we enjoyed the freedom, the sands, and bathing in the sea.

By 1914 my mother was finding life easier. The older members of the family had finished their training and had jobs; Ida had married the year before, and only my brother and I were in school.

I am not sure that my mother had prejudices, but certainly she had many taboos. We were not allowed to go to dances, play cards, go to the theatre and have alcoholic drinks. I could not put her disapproval down to Wesleyan Methodist influence, because she was not a Methodist. Maybe she was trying to prevent her daughters going to the bad. Daughters were not expected to have much life outside the home, but we were never allowed to be idle. My mother and sisters made linen teacloths and tray cloths with drawn-thread work and crochet edging: all diligently hand-made. They made yards and yards of crochet lace, sometimes three to four inches wide which were attached to cloths, towels and pillowcases. I was taught to sew at a very early age, do embroidery and crewel work. However, she did not object to country dancing, so I joined the English Folk Dance Society, and had many happy years going to weekly classes and to the festival every year in the Albert Hall.

Another festival I remember well, was the Whitsun treat: there would be games and races organised by members. We attended a very fashionable and wealthy Wesleyan Methodist Church. Services were three, sometimes four times on Sundays, with meetings throughout the week: Guild, Band-of-Hope (all about temperance), lectures and preparatory sessions for Sunday School teaching: it claimed to have one thousand members. As a family we were involved with all the church activities. We worked hard to raise funds for the National Childrens Home for Methodists, and had a Sewing Meeting once a week to make things for an annual bazaar. When I was older I was put in charge of the Primary Department, an Infants class for the Sunday School. This was all the main part of our lives. Apart from these church associations we had no social life whatsoever. As our parents had no close friends, my mother did not entertain and we were never invited to parties, the church events were central to our lives. All our friendships were there. With our mother's total ban on theatre visits and dances there was little chance of our meeting a young man. However, *one* of our sister's *did* marry: he was the Minister's son, and, of course, they met frequently at the church events (but mostly at our house). Roath Road Methodist Church was very popular. It had a large congregation and when the eminent theologian, Dr. Campbell Morgan came to conduct the Church Anniversary Services, the place was packed and they had to put chairs in the aisles. The secretary of the Sunday School, W.E. Clogg, published a magazine called the *Roath Road News*, which kept people up-to-date with news. Later, when the First World War came it was changed to the *Roath Road Record* and he kept in touch with the boys at the Front.

By the time I was eleven my older sister had left the Higher Grade and gone to a private school, and as I obtained a scholarship to the High School I was allowed to go there. The Third Form was mostly scholarship girls from the Elementary Schools, just like me, whereas the girls from private schools were in the Second Form. There was a distinct difference. For the first few years I was top (or second) of the class, but by the Fifth Form the others of my age had caught up with me and then I was in competition with 'students' and had to work very hard to keep up. I always think that they had a different early training in the private schools (not taught by rote all the time) and this enabled them to approach their studies from a surer angle. Very few of the girls from Elementary Schools reached the Sixth Form or went to university.

I was at Cardiff High School for Girls from 1910 to 1916 and I loved every minute of it. I was so looking forward to going into the Sixth Form, but the War put an end to so many school activities such as the Debating Society, and to many social events. There was a shortage of books too. Several of our mistresses joined the forces and war-work became the first priority. However, we managed to get a good education to prepare us for the next step. My mother found it difficult to make two ends meet with a large family to provide for. Buying books was always a problem, but fortunately, school text books did not change very much and we had to get books second-hand whenever we could. I suppose I was fortunate because I inherited the ones my sisters had used. My childhood had been very sheltered. It was a strict upbringing. When I went to the High School I entered a new world and was surprised to find the liberty that girls of my own age were allowed: I had a lot to learn. In the school library I found books that I would not have dared to take home. Later, when my father found me reading *Tess of the D'urbervilles* by Thomas Hardy, he was very angry and said it was not the sort of book a young woman should read: he found it disgusting.

During the Great War we had a Belgian French mistress at the High School. She formed a group to make knitted things for the troops. I do not think that any effort was made toward preparing us to become 'wives.' The staff were stiff necked spinsters and if they had any romance in their lives, they did not show it. The curriculum was targeted toward scholastic achievement and for many of us that was what we wanted. I can only speak for my own group, but many pupils were quite happy to leave after the Fifth Form. So many of the boys of my age were killed in the War and the chance of marrying was narrowed. I am sure some of the girls had boyfriends but any permissiveness or canoodling in public would be frowned upon. The school hoped to turn out good, well-behaved, moral citizens, leading a useful life.

Cardiff High School was considered an élite, snobbish place, but by the time I arrived, we had girls from every social class in attendance. The Headmistress and staff aimed at giving the girls a fair standard of education. We were prepared for the Junior, Senior and Higher Certificate of the Central Board of Education and hoped to get matriculation. The best achievement was a scholarship to Oxford or Cambridge University. Only a small group reached the Upper Sixth Form, and were mainly those who wanted to have an academic life. The curriculum included cookery, needlework and art, and I thought that these subjects were important because I loved all forms of handicraft. I do not think that we were expected to go on to higher education, but we were given the greatest encouragement if we showed an interest in doing so. Teacher Training College was definitely thought to be *inferior*.

Drama was very important at the High School. The English mistress produced a play every year, and it was given a public performance. Of course, in our family we were *never* allowed to go to the theatre, but I

65

got away with being present by saying that I had to be on *duty*: it was a thrilling occasion for me. Oh! How I longed to be part of it. Unfortunately, the war interrupted my school years: 1914 brought so much change. We had to give up so many things: the Drama Society was one of them. As for games: there were not many facilities for these. We had a hard tennis court and a shared playing field with the Boy's School, but it was a long way away from the school building. I played in the tennis and hockey teams. There was a gymnasium, not very well equipped and a small playground. I imagine that games were not considered important in a girl's school.

I cannot remember many school rules and I certainly did not find them onerous: but then, I like orderliness. Upon reflection, we must have been a tame bunch. There was never any indiscipline, or rebelliousness during my six years at the High School. We were just expected to behave properly and we were so proud of our school uniform that we would not dream of disgracing it. We were not allowed to run in corridors, or up stairs: I think we were expected to be silent. We stopped talking when a mistress came into the form room, but we did not stand up. It was taken for granted that we would be well-mannered and polite: both of which were taught to us at home anyway. I can remember one occasion when I was reprimanded; I had met a Senior Mistress in the town, and of course, I acknowledged her: the next day in school she sent for me and gave me a lesson on deportment. When I think about it, my mother had far more control on my behaviour than did my teachers. I think that we were always under our parents' control, even the ones who left home felt my mother's influence. We knew the rules and took it for granted that we should obey them. I don't think that I ever went out in the evenings without telling my mother when I was going and what time I should be back: even when I was teaching. I rarely went out without one of my sisters. We were never openly rebellious, but there was often friction, and finally my eldest sister left home after a disagreement with my mother.[4]

I never had any contact with boys, apart from my brother's friends: but I wasn't interested in them, so did not seek them out. I would not

[4] This sister worked for the Post Office, and remained unmarried.

have thought it unseemly to sit with a boy I knew on a tram or walk with him in the street. As I was not allowed to go to dances I had no opportunity of meeting boys outside our own particular circle. No mention was made in school of sex, boyfriends, or the dangers of being too intimate: but I think that as a family of girls we were suspicious of men, and our mother's attitude did nothing to disabuse us of this: she did not want us to find husbands. The only boys I knew were either neighbours or friends of my young brother. I took no interest in them and I am sure that my mother gave marriage such a bad name, that we all shied away from it.

We all lived a very sheltered childhood and what were considered unsuitable topics were never discussed in our hearing. We knew nothing about the facts of life or sex (certainly nothing about the 'womanly cycle') and if we asked intimate questions we were told that we would learn when we were older. Pregnant women did not like to be seen in public, especially during the later stage. I remember that my only married sister, Ida, when pregnant, would only go out with her husband at night and that she wore a cloak.

In my childhood there was a horror of infectious diseases: parents were terrified of them. My mother had a remedy for most childish ailments, but if spots came out, she had to send for the family doctor and he had to be *paid*. When I was born, one of my sisters contracted Scarlet Fever and was sent to the sanatorium: the fever hospital. There, she was told by older girls the details of childbirth: she said that it ruined her life and she never forgave me for it. My mother said that if she had been around my sister would never have been sent to the fever hospital and henceforth all illnesses were treated at home. In 1903 my brother also caught Scarlet Fever and the younger members of the family were sent to relatives and friends. I was sent to an aunt and I never forgave my brother for it. The older sisters were allowed to remain at home. A bed was made in the bath and a sheet soaked in disinfectant was hung over the door of the bathroom. Measles was considered to be very dangerous as it could lead to deafness. Fortunately, we all survived.

In 1916, it was time for me to leave the Girls' School. My school record must have been satisfactory as after having matriculated, I was granted a Normal Scholarship to the university. However, I was not what is now called 'university material', as I failed my first year examinations, passing only in English Language and Literature: I was very disappointed and discouraged. I suppose that I could have tried again, but I had wasted a year and did not know whether my scholarship would be renewed. About that period a training department had been established, based upon the Froebel system of education (Kindergarten) and I was offered a transfer to continue my studies in that department: it was a way out and so I gratefully accepted. The course included Child Psychology, Hygiene, English Language (essays), Handicrafts, Music (including country dancing), Teaching of Reading and Simple Arithmetic, Art and Physical Training. The end product was the Higher Certificate of the National Froebel Union and the Teacher's Certificate. I certainly did not choose teacher training for its status of a profession: as teachers we have never been respected and recognised financially for the work we perform. As to a feeling of vocation, it would not have occurred to me that I was doing something 'worthy': there was so little choice.

We all did our teaching practice at the College School: a small private school sponsored by the university staff. I do not remember teaching practice in any elementary school. After I had passed in the examinations, I was appointed as a teacher in the college school, which used kindergarten methods and which had very small classes. I was very happy, but there was no future in it. After a year I got a post at the Alice Ottley School in Worcester.[5] It was a minor public school and was very High Church. I was a Methodist and I did not fit in. The head of the kindergarten department resented my appointment and made my life a misery. She disapproved of my religion, but also objected to my going to services at the cathedral. I was, of course, very inexperienced as a teacher. Fortunately, I was only appointed for a year, but my confidence was completely shattered: I arrived home as a nervous wreck. I felt that I had failed once more.

However, I had to earn my own living, so I pulled myself together and applied for a teaching post in Cardiff. I was immediately appointed as a supply teacher. It was then that I started training as a teacher in earnest. I was sent to various schools to teach all ages and the head

---

[5] When Miss Amor taught in this school in 1922, her salary was sixty pounds per annum.

teachers did not care how inefficient I was, as long as I filled a gap and kept the children under control. Discipline was more important than teaching and the classes were large. In all my time as a school teacher I never had fewer that fifty children in my class (if I had forty-eight, I thought the millenium had come), but at least I had no trouble with discipline and never had to have recourse to harsh methods. I personally deplored the use of the cane and cruel discipline, especially with young children: and I saw plenty of that.

I must have given the impression that I was capable and could get the required results, so that I was left to my own devices, never criticised and allowed to use my own methods. Of course, schools were run on very rigid lines in the 1920s. Rules and regulations were laid down and the syllabus did not leave much to the imagination. The old Victorian buildings were solid and stark, like prisons, very forbidding, especially to small children. The children sat in serried ranks of desks, two to a desk and there was little scope for freedom of movement. The only heating was a coal fire in the corner of the room, but only children who sat in the front row benefited from it and the large rooms were always cold. The playground was tarmaced, very uneven after years of usage and dangerous where slides had been made. The outside lavatories were unhygienic and always wet.

By the time I was given a permanent post techniques were very slowly beginning to change. But even in the 1930s everything was still in short supply: books were very antiquated and dilapidated, materials for art and handicrafts were practically non-existent and it was difficult to break the rigidity of the system. However, I bought reams of cardboard and made apparatus to help with the teaching of reading. I used old slate frames for weaving, and cut up pictures myself to make jig-saws for the children. It was mend and make do, use one's ingenuity, a matter of improvising so that the children could have something interesting to do: all so much effort. This was what it was like for children in the infant schools in the 1920s and 30s.[6]

---

[6] During the summer holidays in 1939, Miss Amor was in Belgium when war broke out. She managed to return home on one of the few passenger boats to cross the channel that August. Miss Amor became Headmistress of Rhydypennau Infants' School.

WILLIAM ARCHIBALD BLADEN OF SWANSEA

Born May 18th, 1899
Son of William Bladen and his wife
Matilda Bladen, née Lewis.

My mother had six sons and three daughters which she raised beyond infancy: two children died when they were babies. I was born at 11 Rutland Street, Swansea. In those days the street was composed mostly of seafaring folk. I started school at eighteen months. It was just across the road. My sister who was three years old had started to attend and took me along as well. She would put me somewhere in the class. We went everywhere together.

There was a strict routine in our house. Each Saturday morning the boy next in line from the one who had started working had to clean all the boots and shoes. He also had to clean the cutlery. You polished the forks and spoons but the knives were cleaned with brick dust on a board. My mother always complained that I never got them clean enough. Then on Monday morning before school we had to set the fire and light the boiler for the weekly wash. When I was a boy one could always earn a few coppers. I'd look out for a lady and carry her bag. There was a regular one who used to give me two eggs for carrying her shopping home. Or I'd go down to Victoria Station and earn a few coppers carrying bags there, and there were always horses to hold for a copper.

Before I left school, probably around the age of twelve, I was employed to take bundles of daily newspapers to the local newsagents. They gave me half a crown a week. After school at around 4.30 p.m. I'd go to Castle Square to get the bundles, which were all labelled and put in a big bag. I also had to carry a bucket of paste to put up posters where permitted. It would take just an hour, the furthest point being Bryn-y-môr Road. Then it was time to play on the street.

At the age of twelve I was in Standard VII which was the last class. At thirteen you took the Labour Exam so that you could leave school.

The youngest boy in the family had to take Dad his pipe and tobacco each evening around six o'clock. He worked as Head Boots at the Metropole Hotel. For this chore we were always given a penny. Father started work at 8.a.m. and at ll.a.m. he came home to change, then he went back and finished the evening about 8 p.m. He received no wages as Head Boots but relied on tips and a fleet of trucks which he owned. The trucks were hired out to the commercial travellers to put their merchandise in. The commercial travellers would come to stay for a week and expect to hire a man to push the truck around the town. For a working class man my father was well off. Before he was fifty he was able to purchase five houses and two farms. When he came home at eight o'clock he'd take his jug to the pub and buy his beer, a bottle of stout for mother and a bar of chocolate for the youngest child. We had all been the lucky child in turn. This was his ritual. As a child I very rarely saw my father. We had to be in bed by the time he came home. Father never touched us, he never punished us; mother would chastise us when needed.

Mother brought up a large family and the only time one could say she showed affection was when we were ill. With the help of my sisters my mother worked from morning till night. We had a three-storey house. My elder brother went to work at the Metropole as a second porter and so slept in; the next boy was working away as an electrician so I don't remember him much. Generally, four of us slept in the attic room; four boys. There was a front parlour which we didn't dare go into. It had to be kept nice in case any of my father's friends called.

For holidays our mother would take us up to Pen-y-bont near Llandrindod Wells to stay with her relatives. When one got to eleven one no longer went with her. My father would go up to vote because he had a farm there. We'd come home and spend the rest of the summer on the sands. I was happy as a child. Our mother used to expect us to do our chores, and I didn't like all the cleaning I had to do on Saturday morning, but I knew it had to be done.

As a child I only went to Sunday School in the afternoon. My parents never made a habit of going to church. My elder brothers and sisters would go to the services at York Place Chapel. When I got home from Sunday School I had to take off my best suit immediately.

Christmas was the happiest time. Father would take us to Studys Roundabout on the Strand. He'd take about eight of us and buy

71

coconuts for all the boys as he couldn't win that number and we'd all go on the roundabouts. One Christmas when I was eleven or twelve there was a man there who could coil wire into the shape of names. I wanted my mother's name coiled for a present, but as neither he nor I could spell Matilda, he had to twist it into 'Mother'.

Football was my hobby. We'd go down to the Recreation Ground. The school had a team. Otherwise we'd play near the sands on the railway sidings.

The Headmaster at Rutland Street School was Mr. Adams, and he used to take snuff whenever he wanted. He would have a large red handkerchief tucked into his shirt when he took it and then have a good sneeze. There was usually snuff in his nostrils. As there were Jewish boys in the school he would exempt them from morning prayers. If I was ever late I used to pretend that I was Jewish and stay with them until prayers had finished. It saved me from getting a row. I loved my masters. They were fair-minded even if they did cane us.

When I was thirteen I left school and as father was Head Porter at the Metropole he got me a job there as a page boy. There was a strict hierarchy amongst the staff there; my father would only eat his food with someone of the same standing. I called him 'Sir' and he addressed me as 'Page.' There was definitely class distinction in hotel life and I didn't really come across it until I became a page. My wages were five shillings a week with food. But on a Tuesday, which was a slack day, I'd have to relieve the Winter Garden waiter and I could then average twenty-five shillings easily in tips. For a boy of fourteen that was as much as a docker was getting for a whole week's work. My hours were 8 a.m. until 3 p.m. and then back again at 5 p.m. until 9 p.m. So there was very little time to spend all that money. In eighteen months I'd saved twenty-five pounds. Yet when I was later apprenticed to a blacksmith I was getting a shilling a week for fifty-four hours work; rising to five shillings a week at the end of the third year.

I only remained a page for eighteen months because the war came. Hotel life changed completely then; the Army seemed to commandeer the place. I had never wanted to be a page. My first ambition was to become a motor mechanic. I went to see the mechanic where they kept the hotel bus and asked if I could come and work with him. He said, "Go and ask your father." But when I asked for his consent he thundered out "Those stinking bloody things won't last five minutes." He favoured horses and saw no future for me working as a mechanic.

In 1916 my father retired at the age of fifty-six; he had had a good life at the hotel. The tips were good and with the hiring of trucks as well he was earning more in a year than the Chief Constable of Neath. Even in those days he was paying income tax. They all did well at the Metropole—the Head Waiter eventually owned several hotels in Brighton—and the man that followed my father had to pay two pounds a week for the post.

We joined my mother at Leasom Well Farm near Llanrhidian; I was seventeen then and working with a Gower blacksmith. My father thought that horses would always be necessary. They would go on being used forever; I would never be without a job.

ANNIE MILES OF PONTRHYDYFEN, GLAMORGAN.

Born February 18th, 1899
Daughter of Evan Miles and his wife
Mary Miles, née Lewis.

The first memory I have is of being taken to visit my grandmother. I may have been fifteen months old. I remember sitting on my father's lap by the bedside of an old lady with a bonnet on her head. She was sitting up in bed and she gave me an orange. I was born in Pontrhydyfen in 4, Penrhys Villas now called 13 Twynypandy. My father sold the house and we moved to Bryn Anchor—9, Morgan's Terrace—because my parents had been grieved at the loss of their eldest son, Edwin Morgan Miles. He had suffered from meningitis. When he died they were heartbroken. So I and my two sisters moved to Bryn Awelon. Both my sisters were older than me, Jennette Mary and Eveline were their names.

One thing I remember when I was getting on for five was the religious revival.[1] I remember it vividly. There was a great excitement one Sunday. It was said that Evan Roberts was coming to Jerusalem Methodist Chapel that evening. There were crowds of people gathered as they walked to the place of worship. The chapel was full; the galleries and all the downstairs were absolutely full to its limit. There was a great deal of singing hymns and shouts of Hallelujahs and praying for forgiveness. After an hour and a half of waiting the Revivalist came and went up to the pulpit. He started to pray but there was so much singing and praising that he could not go on. He simply walked back and fore in the pulpit hitting his right fist into his left palm and moving his head under intense emotion. The girls in front of me in the gallery stretched forward. There was a commotion downstairs. Someone had been taken ill. I asked the one in front what was wrong. She said "Elizabeth Evans' mother has had a fit." After a while, after watching

---

[1] In the autumn of 1904, a former collier at the Broadoak Colliery near Loughor, Evan Roberts, started a preaching mission which triggered what became known as *The Revival*: a period when evangelical preachers sought to revitalise religion in Wales. Evan Roberts was a Methodist preparing for the ministry at Newcastle Emlyn. Some chapels held all night vigils.

the men in the gallery bursting out singing "Tell mother I'll be there"; "Hold out the life-line, someone is sinking today", I saw my father at the top of the stair beckoning me and so he took me home. The following evening, after tea on Monday, I had changed into my playing pinafore (my school pinafore was worn only for school), I remembered the previous Sunday evening and wondered if anything was happening at the chapel. I wandered down to the chapel and saw the minister Ambrose Williams leading the faithful band of worshippers from the prayer meeting. I walked alongside until they came to a building which had been a house, but was now a Conservative Club. There was a big window at the top floor and men with beer glasses sitting there. Mr. Ambrose Williams began to preach and pray. In a few minutes the drinkers began to laugh and jeer and one man threw his beer toward the protestors. This insult daunted them and they went away.

The Revival had a strange effect on me. If I wanted to amuse my sisters I would close my eyes and move my head from side to side and beat my right fist into the palm of my left hand. I always got a laugh. I used to go on my knees at the bottom of the stairs and imitate prayers. I would sit behind the kitchen door and do likewise. Then I would go sometimes to my friend Lavinia and her brother Oswald to play in their cellar. We would play prayer meeting. Lavinia and I pretended to sing hymns. Oswald would close his eyes and pray. I knew then I did not have the right words, but they sounded like them. There was one boy who wanted his cat saved and after that he was called "Save the cat" (in Welsh, *Achub y gath*). Children played prayer meeting in the quarry, but I refused to go to that.

Later my father built a new house, there were two together, he was a builder and miner. There were four bedrooms in this house, and it had a big garden. During the spring we children had to help with the gardening. My father dug the garden and made furrows. We children had a stick about seven inches long and placed bits of potatoes with eyes in the furrows that had been scattered with dung. My father then would close the furrows. My mother's job was to cut the potatoes in shapes to secure the eyes for growth. We children sometimes were sent to gather dung left on the hillside, but usually we ordered a ton because horses were the carriers then.

Everybody kept two pigs. Then at the end of summer, they would be killed and we had plenty of bacon hanging from the hooks in the scullery or kitchen. It was fun watching the butcher killing our pig after having chased him if he escaped screaming. We watched the knife thrust in the pig's neck and the blood squirting out without flinching. The dead pig would be cut up into pieces. Some parts were sent to neighbours to repay similar gifts. The pig would be salted on a stone table. That night we would enjoy the faggots of liver and onions: one tin was kept for the neighbours and we had the other tin of faggots for supper. Delicious.

As we grew up we had a very active winter in chapel work. On Monday evenings the parents went to Prayer Meeting while we played. I remember there was an old tree at the roadside where we smaller children gathered round a teenager who would tell us ghost stories. On a Tuesday evening we would have a Bible class preparing us for the Bible examinations in March. The youngest children would be examined in the Catechism For Children by Thomas Charles of Bala. On a Wednesday evening we would have a singing practice for a concert in April. The concert was held in the chapel and a stage fixed up for the purpose. The older people and some youngsters had singing practice to learn an oratorio—perhaps *The Messiah* or *Creation*—there were well known artists to sing the arias. On the Thursday evening there was a society meeting where the children had to recite a verse from the Bible and were questioned about it. We spent Sunday in religious work: at nine o'clock there was an hour of prayer for young boys to prepare themselves to later take part in prayer meetings. Then at ten-thirty a service. At two o'clock it was time for Sunday School where we all sang children's hymns for the Singing Festival in March or April. In Sunday School we children learned a children's catechism and the older ones had another catechism with questions and answers on Bible ethics. My father was a highly religious man. He went to chapel services, Sunday school, prayer meetings and the society meetings of a religious group. He prayed night and morning. He read the Bible almost every day: it was daily on the table in the kitchen. He *did* like the religious fervour of the Revival. When there was singing and praising in the vestry he went out to the front and read from St. Paul:

"Be temperate in all things." An excitable congregation prayed aloud for him to be saved—I remember it vividly.

Tuesday evening was an important night for us as we would go to the vestry to be taken by Mr. Ambrose Williams. He spoke of Temperance. We had to sign a card and we were given it to keep. The card was very pretty, being decorated with painted flowers. It was signing the pledge to be a teetotaller. Then we had brooches given us, white ones in the form of a bow with the letters U.D.M.D.—*Undeb Merched y De* (The South Wales Women's Union): a temperance branch.

Whitsun was a special treat. We marched on Whit Monday and sang three or four hymns. All the Welsh chapels joined in, Methodists, Baptists and Independents. At one time we had a village band to lead us. Then after marching through the village, a speech was given by one of the chosen members as to the meaning of Whitsun. We would then return to our village chapels for tea and cake. In the evening we would all meet in a field, both old and young, to have games such as *March* and *Kiss in the Ring*: the man in the centre of the ring would make things up and when he used the word "March" everyone changed partners. The one who failed to do this would have to go to the centre and repeat the game. After games the people would go to their individual chapels to enjoy a concert—sometimes they were competitive and members might have to read a paragraph without stops for breath or grammar, or maybe compete in reciting verse beginning with a certain letter or competitions on a love letter, and, of course, there would be singing contests.

As I grew older, say seven or eight years of age, the village grew and strangers came to live in the community from England: the Belchers, Pattersons, Pitts, Halleys and Wheelers. One girl, Maud, became my friend and another, Pat, of these English people. They went to church rather than chapel and caused the church to become English eventually. There was some conflict, I believe, but the English had their way. Of course, we three[2] were in the majority still. The church never marched with the Sunday Schools on Whit Monday. They went to Margam Castle, and had their tea there. When the English children came to the village, play changed a great deal. Now we were shown how to attach a

---

[2] Annie means Methodists, Baptists and Independents.

stone to a cotton and hang it on a door, unrolling the cotton and hide while pulling the cotton until the stone tapped upon the wood and drew the occupiers to the door. They had skates which I borrowed. They made fun of our Welsh and our accent although they were not good at schoolwork although it was all in English.

The English girl Winnie Wheeler taught us about Mesmerism. She got one of our friends to lie down, close her eyes, and put her fingers in her ears. Then Winnie proceeded to move her hands over the girl's closed eyes. The girl, after a while, got up, quite white, and began rushing around. She came to the brink of the quarry: we hit her hard on her back and she came back to herself. I never wanted that experience again.

Three English families came to live next door to us. The Piggotts from Lancashire were the first. They did not stay very long because they imagined a kind of knocking at night and they were superstitious. They introduced us to fireworks on Guy Fawkes Night and they shared out jelly and blancmange to the children. We had never before celebrated Guy Fawkes. An English custom. I do not remember any bonfires at all. Our celebration was *Nos Calon* or All Saints when we played "ducking apples." There would be a big earthenware tub full of water with apples floating in it: my father urged us to catch one by the mouth only. The Piggotts wore clogs. They were very friendly. Then the Jenkins family came. The eldest son was Harold and although he was fourteen years old he used to cry when he had a bath. They stayed a couple of years and moved to Aberavon. Then came Mr. and Mrs. Addis who were childless and made a great fuss of me and called me their foster daughter. Mrs. Addis suffered from some skin trouble if she used water a great deal, so I helped her with the housework. I used to wash the scullery, pantry, kitchen and passage and steps every Saturday morning. She gave me one shilling, but when she discovered that my mother kept the money she gave me one penny for myself. Before she left in 1913, to move to Port Talbot, she took me one Christmas to London for three weeks to stay with her sister. I was taken to see a pantomime—*Aladdin*—for the first time: the main song was 'Joshua, Joshua.' I was taken to see the Houses of Parliament and I remember pointing out the sculpture of Queen Boadicea.

As a family, our interests were solely round chapel life. Of course, we children could play on Penrhys Mountain and could hide under a huge crag when it rained. Our games were making a house with bits of stones and china—fireplace, scullery, parlour. We played Jack Stones and Buttons. We gathered reeds on top of the hill and made rattles (with a stone inside) and a whip. There was a great "make believe" in our activities. We imitated older people: mimicking them. Very often we would find a dead bird. We would make a grave and encircle it with stones and plant a flower and then walked in twos to the grave.

On top of Penrhys where the ruined house stood there was a stream. The farmers dammed the stream and we would watch them washing the sheep and then shear them. We loved going across the mountain overlooking the village to the ruined chapel, Gyfylchi, which previously had been an Anglican church. We would go up to a farm (where they were related to us) to help stack the corn and also make haycocks in the fields. We had tea after this. There were boys on the farm and they used to give us rides on the gambo. If the bottom of the gambo had been repaired the boys would take us over the rough ground and we would scream because the boards would pinch us as we sat on them. We had a short ride on the horses backs—rarely though—because we were always busy there. The daughter used to milk the cows and if we went too, she would turn the cow's teat and spray us with the cow's milk. The boys and girls would sit in the turnip field and share a turnip between us: strangely enough, we never had indigestion.

I remember a sad event in my life. I lost my little sister Edith Irene. I used to look after her. She was very frail. She had blond hair and blue eyes and very pink cheeks: her legs were so thin and so were her arms. I remember her having a woollen shawl on her back often. It was my job to take her to school. Every morning she used to cry and made me late for school. Once I said resentfully "Oh dear" and then took her to school. I regretted that resentment very much because she died soon afterwards: she had diphtheria. I remember I had to run down to the surgery to get something for the doctor who had come in to attend to her. She was lying on a bed in the middle room and I could watch from the doorway. My father and mother were there with the doctor. I watched the doctor: I saw him operate on her throat. She turned her head to the right and passed away. I knew she had died. I went out to the back yard and lay on the ground crying helplessly. After the tears passed away I got up and went to the scullery. My mother was washing a garment and was crying and moaning at the same time. My father was there trying to console her. It was the second child she had lost.

On the day of Edith's funeral all of us girls went in new black frocks trimmed with white braid and my brother had a black suit. On the following Sunday evening we all went to our seat in the chapel. After a death in the family, all stayed at home on the first Sunday: but I believe we went. We would remain seated all during the service: we did not get up to sing because we were recent mourners. We wiped our eyes with black-fringed handkerchiefs. Then on the third Sunday you could get up and join in the singing if you felt like it. As for the black mourning frock, I wore it as a school frock. When someone died there would be a *Gwyl Nos*: a vigil. My granny took me to one once in Pont Du, near Port Talbot, when her sister's daughter had died. And I remember once going with a number of children to see an old man in his coffin: it was customary. However, he was the only one I remember going to see, because some girls asked me to go with them. His widow took us up to the bedroom to see him. I can remember now what he looked like, with a small beard.

An important figure in our lives was my maternal grandmother who lived with us. She had kept a china shop at *Cwmafon* where my mother was born. My grandfather had emigrated with his two sisters to Ohio and died there. Granny had refused to go. So my mother was brought up by her grandparents. My maternal great-grandmother had come from a farm in Morriston: she had had seven brothers and each one had a son as clergyman. I was very fond of my Granny Lewis. She always read the New Testament: it was kept on a bracket above her head in her bedroom. She taught us our letters from the big letters at the beginning of a chapter. She also encouraged us by giving us biscuits in letter form: if we knew them we had them to eat. Later, when I could read well, she used to call me every night on my way to bed and asked me to read a chapter or a psalm from the New Testament. She loved Corinthians 13:

There remaineth three things,
Faith, hope and charity.

I used to comb Granny Lewis's hair and put a fresh cream collar on her frock as she sat by the fireside. She was fond of flowers and in our garden she planted dahlias, tiger lilies, peony and pansies. She grew chives, mint and red and black currants. But she used to have heart attacks. I remember once when she was ill I got up even before my mother did. Mother attended to her, and I went to call the doctor who lived next door. I shouted, "Doctor, doctor, Granny is ill."

He came and went into her bedroom while I shivered on the stairs, waiting. She had taught us all a prayer which hung up on the wall in her bedroom and I have always said it,

> O Lord, our Heavenly Father
> Teach me how to pray.
> Make me sorry for my faults
> And forgive me for all that I have
> Done amiss this day.
> Bless my father and mother,
> Brothers and sisters and take them all
> Into thy Holy keeping this night
> For the sake of Jesus Christ,
>   Amen.

My grandmother died in 1914 from a heart attack. By then I was fifteen. She helped to teach me my prayers, and she had introduced me to the Bible. It was she and my parents who gave us all our standards. They set the seal on our lives.

It was when I was four and a half that I started school. My mother and father had gone to Aberavon on business. My eldest sister, who was six years older than me, decided I should go to school with her in the afternoon. She put a coat on me and I remember she put my blue knitted gaiters on me, too. The headmistress was Mrs. Lewis, my mother's uncle's wife, and when I was in the second class, a girl, Lavinia Williams, with whom I played quite a lot, bit my hand and the marks of her teeth were deep. I went out to Mrs. Lewis who sat at a desk and showed her my hand. She called Lavinia out and raised her scissors which hung around her waist and said that if Lavinia did that again, she would take her teeth out with the scissors. In the big school we were all taught in one large room: there were standards up to nine all together. I had an experience in the big school. Boys used to "mitch" from school. They would leave the playground in the afternoon play and run up the mountainside towards Bryn. Once I was hit by a snowball with a stone in it thrown from the boys' playground. The cloakroom was at the entrance to the big room and sometimes we were taken there for reading: it was in English, of course. We had singing lessons altogether since all the classes were in the big room. I remember learning,

> Roses white and roses red,
> What a pretty show
> Wreathed around her pretty head
> For a show, you know.

But they did teach us Welsh songs too. The master, who was my mother's uncle, had his desk facing the whole school. He always had a cane to hand. If boys were late they were put in a row and received a cane on the hand. The master sometimes inspected our shoes which he commanded to be cleaned every day and he made us raise our hands to see if they had been washed. He always took us for prayers in the morning. During "times table" we all had to join in, and spelling, too, was all simultaneous, in a sing-song fashion, it was all like incantation.

There was a room, smaller, at the other end of the big room where I remember having sewing. The sewing consisted of patches for darning specimens and oversewing and tucking together. It was the master's job to train the student teachers. He used to go at seven o'clock each morning to the school and take them in English and Arithmetic. His wife, Headmistress of the Infant's School, took them in needlework and Infant work. Those girls who wanted to teach did not go to college because of marriage prospects.

A new school opened in 1907: we had mugs as gifts and a picture card of the school which had separate rooms now for each class. In Standard IV a local teacher, Miss Thomas, taught poems in Welsh. In the next class, Standard V our teacher was a Mr. Thomas. He was bald, and some children called him *Baldhead*, but I never did so. He was always immaculate—fine tweed suits and very white collars and he was so very clean. He was a good teacher. One girl, Winnie Wheeler, English, was very precocious. Mr. Thomas had a habit of calling the girls by their surnames. He called her Wheeler: the girl got up and said "I have a handle to my shovel," meaning she had a Christian name as well. He was highly amused, but did not change the habit. There was another incident too. A boy called Harry Jones became aggressive and threw an inkwell at Mr. Thomas: it missed him and went on the wall behind him. I remember the ink trickling down. I saw a girl rushing out of the room and I went with her. Soon we went back. Mr. Thomas looked amusingly at us and said "Where have you been?" I felt very silly and went back to my place. Then he went to get the headmaster who had his cane with him. The master was very short, but everyone was afraid of him. He spoke to Mr. Thomas and Harry Jones. The latter said something and Mr. Thomas slapped his face. The master told the boy to hold out his hand and he had the cane on each hand and was told to go back to his place.

Mr. Thomas tried to teach us social behaviour. For example, he once said "If I were to meet a friend and one of you was with me, if I said 'Have you met my friend before?' what would you say?" Of course, I was quick to reply "Oh! No, Mr. Thomas," with a very snobby accent, I thought. He smiled and said that the right reply was "I have not had the pleasure."

Now I became of age to try the scholarship. There was a written examination and having passed that, one had to have an interview in an oral exam. The morning of the examination I stayed a little longer in bed because I had only to catch the ten o'clock. An order came from school that I must attend before catching my train. There was a rush of activity and I turned up at school rather late. Mr. Thomas had asked questions, and answers had been given before I arrived. As soon as I got in Mr. Lewis at once pointed at me and asked "What is the meaning of Pontrhydyfen?" I was not able to answer straight away: he

83

slapped my face and said "You'll fail." It had a terrible effect upon me. He had discussed that, no doubt, before I came into the room. I have never forgotten that insult. However, I won the scholarship and started at the Aberavon County School at the age of eleven and a half years. They were happy years. The year was 1910, the end of Edward VII's reign. By this time my father was politically minded, and fought the Council Elections. I read some pamphlets he had by Keir Hardie.

Christmas was a happy time. We would all hang up our stockings. By the morning we would have an apple, an orange, nuts and sweets in the stocking. We were also given one shilling each to buy anything we wanted in Aberavon: I always bought a lot of things at tuppence each. Once my father bought a toy that could be wound on the table and move along: and I remember a Christmas when there was a Chinaman, with his tin plait, moving over the table. Another time a swan with wings flapping as well as moving, after turning a screw. Oh! And the tying of the puddings was quite a ceremony which my father performed while we children watched. Then the bubbling water as the puddings were placed in the boiling water and making sure of the time taken to boil. Then we loved watching the yeast cakes being prepared and we had to take stalks from the fruit and currants. We always had a goose for Christmas because my mother liked to have a supply of goose grease for sore throats: it was placed on strips of flannel and wrapped around our necks. It was at Christmas time boys used to come early in the morning to wish us a "Happy Christmas." On New Year's morning a cousin of ours with black hair would be allowed to come in at six o'clock in the morning to wish us all a "Happy New Year." One Christmas morning, when I was still quite young, my grandmother woke me up to go to the *Plygain* on Christmas morning at our Sunday School *Y Gangen*. I recited the verses from the New Testament about Christ's birth, from Matthew: my grandmother had taught me these. I still recall holding my grandmother's arm and looking up at the stars: "Which one is the Star of Jesus?" I asked. "Oh! The bright one," said my grandmother. After returning home at seven o'clock my father was very annoyed that I had been taken from my bed so early in the morning: I never went again until I was grown-up.

I have tried to recall some of my clothes as a child. We were three girls and, of course, when we were very young one frock passed to the next after a few alterations. When my clothes were new they were worn only on a Sunday, until I grew out of them. They were lengthened for school, and later used only for play. White pinafores were worn for school and dark navy patterned ones for play. There was a village dressmaker who made all our clothes. My eldest sister became apprenticed to her, and after 1910 my sister made all our clothes. She made a tussore silk suit for my baby brother and he disliked it. He also had a velvet suit, trousers, and smock. My older brother wore a Norfolk jacket. During the winter we wore woollen clothes. I remember having a knitted blue woollen coat. Of course, the underwear for we girls consisted of a calico chemise, ribbed corset, a flannel petticoat—either white for best or red for every day—black woollen stockings to above the knees and boots. In summer the underwear might be flannelette. There was always worn a white petticoat of calico over the flannel or flannelette petticoat.

Every Monday, all the Sunday clothes would be brushed and put away for the following Sunday. All the Sunday shoes were also cleaned and put away. There was a big mahogany chest of drawers on the landing and this was the place where our best clothes were kept.

There are so many things that flood into my mind when I think about those days. My mother made all her own bread: the dough was put into tins with her initials dented out on the outside of the tin. My mother would take the tins each week to the village bakehouse kept by the grocer. On Friday evenings we children would go with an older cousin to fetch the loaves: I loved the crust hanging over the edge of the tin. When we were ill we were given senna tea. There were only paraffin lamps to light our darkened streets. My father laid water-pipes from our allotment to both houses where we lived. There was plenty of water from the reservoir on the hill: this was piped too, down to the roadside where there were taps for the village people at various points. People could also get water from a well above Jerusalem Chapel. Once there was a carnival, and Mrs. Matherson, the doctor's wife, took part as Britannia: she was on horseback with a shield, red, white and blue, a rod and a crown: she was dressed in white. We were taken as children to the fair in Neath: once a year in September. I loved to get up early on the Thursday to watch the farmers going to the cattle fair. The horses were adorned with red, white and blue ribbands, plaited manes and tails. I remember the first occasion putting on a pretty frock before everyone else had awakened: I called out a song of the fair and the farmers threw pennies and halfpennies on the the lawn in front of our house. That was before I started school. On the Saturday evening of the fair, my parents would take us and we would walk to Neath, four miles away. We enjoyed the shows, especially the dancing girls with high boots and frilly frocks. There were moving pictures. The journey home was tiring, but my brother was carried part of the way on my father's back.

During the 1914-1918 war, the men teachers left for the army. There was a shortage of staff in our schools. At my grammar school there were sixth form pupils who were prepared to go in for a teaching career. We had all passed our Junior Certificate which had to be taken in Form V: those who failed this had to leave school. Those of us in Form VI who said we would become teachers, were given ten pounds by the local authority (my mother bought me a gold pendant out of the money). We could not take a teaching post until we were seventeen years of age. I passed at fifteen, so it meant a year of private study at school, and then followed the Student Teacher year: it was now 1915 and the middle of the war. I started teaching in my home village for one and a half days a week, for which I received ten shillings. Then progressed to Student Teacher status, which meant teaching observation, except on Wednesdays and Friday afternoons when we had to attend the Grammar School. During the observation year we had to teach four lessons, either on Nature, Geography or History. These lessons had to be written down in an orderly way with *Introduction and Apparatus, Presentation* and *Recapitulation*. The class teacher was present to criticise. The headmaster looked over the written lesson before it was given. I had a few education books from the former headmaster who was my relative.

At this village school there were over sixty children in the class I observed most of the time. There was corporal punishment administered almost daily. The teacher was untrained and had come straight from grammar school. The headmaster caned boys and girls who were late in the morning: they were lined up in the hall. This was generally accepted by everybody.

After my year's probation period of observation I had a job at the school and was given Standard II. My friend had been an observer in the Infant's School; because of that the headmaster decided to join the boys of Standards I and II together, and my friend had that age group with girls. It meant that my class was eighty-four pupils and my friend had sixty: it was hard work every day.

There were a lot of lessons called "simultaneous": this meant teaching tables and spelling, daily, almost. We gave Religious Instruction and recited psalms each morning. After one month, the headmaster put the girls and boys of Standard I together, and I had the boys and girls of Standard II. The war seemed to go on and on. We had to be very economical with the materials we had. Every line in a book had to be filled up by the children before another one was given out. It was the same with arithmetic books: absolutely no wasted space. Every page had to be filled to its capacity. It was painful where pens and nibs were concerned. Children had a habit of pressing the nibs and this would cause a space on the nib: I spent a lot of overtime straightening them out for the following morning. There were also to be *absolutely* no *blots* on the paper. It was a constant strain I can tell you: every book was carefully examined by the headmaster before a new one was issued, and perhaps we were given half a dozen nibs when we needed many more. There were two large classes in the hall because of the population explosion. After two years of this gruelling work I went to Swansea Training College. It was 1918, the end of the war, and I was just nineteen years. I was going to be a properly trained teacher and after two years would return to Pontrhydyfen School.

CISSIE EVERETT OF CROSS KEYS, MONMOUTHSHIRE

Born February 7th, 1900
Daughter of Albert James Everett and his wife
Eliza Jane Everett, née Guy.

When I was born my father was a soldier in South Africa and was later at the relief of Mafeking in May of that year. I was born in Salisbury Street, Cross Keys near Newport, and was nearly two years old before my father came home. When he did get back he was chosen to guard Queen Victoria's body at her lying-in-state. He always maintained it was the hardest job he'd ever done—two hours on and two hours off—without moving a single bit. Then he left the army and became a miner.

We were ten children and I was the second eldest. My sister was a year and ten months older. We moved from Salisbury Street to Halls Road Cottages which belonged to the Railway. My mother lost me one morning when I was three years old because my sister had taken me to school with her, and I just stayed. I liked school. The head-mistress's name was Miss Bashum, which didn't seem funny then, but it does upon reflection. There were other small kids in the class. Families were so large in those days it was a relief to mothers to have them taken off to school at the earliest chance. There was probably another baby in the family. The women had one after another.

As children we weren't expected to do much in the house, except carry water from a continual running spout from the mountain. We kept a tub under it which was always full of water. There was no gas or electric in the house, just a double burner oil lamp. My mother used to do paper-hanging to make extra money. She could get up and out to paper two bedrooms before coming back to send us off to school. That was women's work, paper-hanging. They were good at it, and it helped to buy things they needed.

One Sunday morning as a 'jaunt' we were taken down by one of the managers to cut coal in my father's heading. There was nothing special about Sunday in our house. They didn't go to chapel; Dad would go down to the Conservative Club for an hour around half past eleven. When I was around ten years of age I decided myself that I'd like to go to Hope Baptist's Sunday School because my friends were going. We only had four rooms in our house and there was no pleasure at home, it was better at Sunday School. You could have some peace and quiet at Sunday School. It was just an hour, but worth it for the change. And the Sunday School teachers were kind and nice to you: they didn't shout. They made you feel wanted. There was very little to do at Cross Keys. On Tuesdays there was Band of Hope and this also helped to make my life a bit more interesting. To say life was dreary was an understatement. There were so many of us at home, all crammed into that tiny cottage. And there was too many of us for Mam to take an interest: it was drudgery for her, too.

The only time my father ever hit me was with a kipper; I suppose it was the only thing handy. I can't remember what I'd done. My mother would be the one to hit us and she had hard hands. She worked extremely hard, looking after us, and also wallpapering for our neighbours. Perhaps the only pleasure she had was going up to the Cross Keys Hotel for a glass of whisky. If she had a baby in arms she'd hide it under her cape so no-one would see. A noggin of whisky was a shilling, and she'd enjoy it. My parents never went out together. He'd go down to the Club and she'd stay in. I suppose she always had a baby to look after. Parents did separate things in those days. There'd be other women up in the hotel, so Mam could have a natter. I suppose it was the only bit of pleasure she got.

About four times a week my Granny Davies, my mother's mother, used to come down to the bridge steps and call up. One of us would go to see what she wanted: usually it was all her fresh crusts, well-buttered and wrapped up as a special treat for me. I was her favourite, so for me sometimes it would even be cakes. You can't imagine what a treat it was. Cake wasn't served very much in our Mam's kitchen, so Granny Davies's scraps were seen as luxuries. It was the only time I could really taste the butter on anything.

There were no such things as holidays. But once a year we all went on an outing with the Conservative Club to Barry Island. There would be lots to do, with the fair and the water. It was a big day. Perhaps the only time we ever left Cross Keys. We'd make the most of it, pray for good weather, for the sun to be out.

We were so many at home, all crammed into two bedrooms. My elder sister went to live with grandmother and when my Aunt Annie got married she went to live there instead. To break the monotony of life we'd play 'Cati' down the Dram Road. You took a stick about six inches long and round, and knock one end with another stick to see how far you could send it. There was also 'Bowly'; a hoop and a stick which you could run along with. When we played skipping at school I would never take my turn at skipping because I wore men's boots which mother had been given. I always stayed turning the rope. You can't imagine how ashamed I felt. There I was, a girl, wearing a big pair of men's boots. There was so many us, all needing something on our feet. It was a struggle on the wages that the men got, and ten kids cost a lot to keep in footwear.

When I was thirteen years old I started to work at the Conservative Club; getting in every morning at 6 a.m. to do the cleaning. I was the only cleaner there, doing all the work for five shillings a week. It was my father who asked if I would do, because they couldn't get anyone and he was a regular customer there. So it was me to do all the slaving away after the boozers the night before. A thirteen year old girl doing all the washing and scrubbing of the floors, scrubbing away on my hands and knees. My mother took the five shillings and gave me a penny. If I hadn't spent the penny by Monday she'd have that as well. One morning the Headmaster saw that my pinafore was wet and dirty and called me into his room. He asked me why I didn't wash before coming to school. I told him that I had to go out to work first. He was very nice about it, but said "You may as well leave school because you can't do two jobs." I was only at the Club nine months.

At the age of fourteen I went to the Green Meadow Public House as general dogsbody, doing all the donkey work. At first I received twenty-five shillings a month, then they said they'd raise it to thirty-shillings to be paid the first of each month. I was caught out there because some months have five weeks. And it was hard work I can tell you. They expected a lot out of girls then. I was thin as a rake and yet expected to do all the heavy work. My life just seemed to be a bit of sleep and endless hours of work.

Each day I cleaned the public bars, the cellar, did the washing and part of the cooking and looked after the five children. It was a live-in job and it was necessary for me to sleep with two of the children as they only had three bedrooms. I got up about 7 a.m. with Mrs. Mogford and started to get the children ready for school. That wasn't easy with five of them to wash, dress and give a bit of breakfast to; but it was better than slaving away in the bars, and down in the cellar. That came after they were sent off to school.

It was like slavery at the Green Meadow, the only comfort I had in life was going to Band of Hope on Tuesdays, choir practice on Wednesday and Christian Endeavour on Friday. Life would have been one grinding round of work if it hadn't been for these evenings in the chapel. It seems strange now, but I was working in a pub and yet President of Band of Hope. I didn't drink and looked forward to these meetings very much. The pub remained my home until I was eighteen and the Great War had finished.

It wasn't much of a childhood looking back. Our parents had no time for us. And really, I was shoved out to work as soon as it could be done, to bring in a bit of money. Then when the chance came to have me live-in somewhere, at the Green Meadow Pub, they grabbed at the chance: it reduced the number of children at home. The sooner you could get out, go away, especially girls as live-in domestics, the better it was for families. There was no joy in my childhood, not what you would call a happy time.

HERBERT JAMES SMITH OF ABERTILLERY

Born June 29th, 1909
Son of Herbert James Smith and his wife
Ruth Smith née Chivers.

Although my mother had been born in Blaina near Nant-y-glo in 1892, she met my father when she was in service in London. A lot of Monmouthshire girls went to the big houses in London as maids. She didn't speak much Welsh as Monmouthshire was under the jurisdiction of the English. Our father had been born in 1890 in Leicester. When they got married they were still in their teens. Mam was seventeen and Dad was nineteen. I was their first child, born in London, but when I was about six months old they decided to come to Wales. Dad was to find work in the mines in Abertillery.

Our grandfather on the Chivers side had been a miner since the age of nine. That's when he started, as a little boy, down the mines. He had to get up at the crack of dawn, 5am. to walk fifteen miles in order to be there for 7am. Now and again, if he was lucky, he'd get a lift in a horse and cart. In those days the mines took girls, too, at fifteen, but they were kept on the surface: sorting out the coal on the top. This grandfather must have been pretty fit: he was ninety-five when he died, after working for sixty years as a miner.

Mam was to have six children, three boys and three girls. I was dressed in frocks until the age of four, then breeched. That was usual for all boys. She never *said* she was pregnant: the baby just arrived. We would notice Mam was pregnant when she cut the bread, because it was picked up, the loaf, and held into the body, and then cut. Only the midwife delivered the babies, Nurse Reed. We would be sent up, one of us, to get her: saying "Mam's ill." That's what we were told to tell her. It was never "The baby's coming." Our conversation at home was never on personal things, *never*. So nothing was ever said. The midwife came to deliver the baby, but she could also be sent for to lay out the dead. That would be her job, too. Mind, during the war some women learned a bit of medical knowledge in the Medical Corps, and so after the war they would lay out the dead: people would go to them. But also the local midwife, even if she did charge a bit more, probably not much more. There was very little money around and so people tried to save on funeral expenses whenever they could: every penny was precious. Accidents with the doctor called had to be avoided at all costs. For sprains there was a liniment, an embrocation which could be bought from a local man: he also looked after you. He would have a reputation and people would go to him for help. For a sprain he would take you up to a mountain spring, stone cold it was, and put your arm or leg under the water.. That would put you right. Ice-cold that water was, even in summer.

Our religion was Primitive Methodists, and we went to Tabernacle. We children went regularly to chapel on a Sunday afternoon because we were each given an attendance card. If you went regularly you would get a free ticket to Barry Island on the Sunday School Outing. We all went by train. About fifty of us. It was a great day out at the sea. No one wanted to miss *that*. But we were all very pious in our community. You daren't put a foot wrong—even if you wanted to—for fear of gossip. They would talk, the neighbours. Nobody wanted to go the wrong way.

Mam never drank. Never. Her family were dedicated church people. And, anyway, she couldn't afford to. There was no spare money for that. Our house had been built for the miners: it was a two up and two down affair. We had a cold water tap in the pantry which had a big slab of stone in it, always cool, well, most of the time. Under the slab we kept a bucket. There was no sink. We were lucky to have a cold water tap inside. Dishes were washed in a bowl. When we went outside to the lav' we had to take a bucket of water with us so that we could throw it down the lav' and flush everything away. Our house had stone stairs up to the two bedrooms and they were very cold stairs. Most of us had chilblains.

Mam went in for wine-making. This was done in a large earthenware pot, huge it was, twelve to eighteen inches in diameter (you could make bread in it) red and very thick. This was used to make the wine. It was placed beside the fire in order to ferment, with a piece of toast swimming on the surface, with a bit of fresh yeast on top of the toast. A cloth was placed over the pot and it was left for some time.

When it wasn't used for wine-making, the bread was kept in it as it had a lid to it. It was a cool pot, made of terracotta: we never had bread covered in mildew. The nettle wine Mam made was said to be good for rheumatism. It was all said to be for medicinal reasons. But it was a cheap way to get merry, later, when we were young men. We would gather together with a bottle of parsnip wine, take a little tot each, make the bottle last a couple of nights, and play cards. It was potent stuff. We would go outside and the air would hit us as we left the house.

If anyone called at a home—knocked on the door—and you went to open the door, if it was a man he would always say "Is the boss in?" And they'd mean the husband. No one thought of the wife as having any power. The dad was boss. It was an acknowledged fact. Mam would go out shopping once a week only, for the main groceries. If something else was needed during the week, one of us children went for it. So the only time she went out seemed to be once a week to do the shopping. Mam seemed like a prisoner: tied to the home. The men got paid on a Saturday; then they went drinking first: that was what they all did. Then Mam got whatever money was left over. The miner got 2s.10d. a top, so wages fluctuated, and so did the money my mother got. She never *did* know how much to expect week by week. The miner had to pay his *butty* (the boy who helped him) and so it took up part of his wages. Dad did buy us a radio before it was common in most homes. And Mam had a sewing machine so she could make clothes for us. When we came to Whitsun time everybody had to have something new. All the women would be busy making things for the Whitsun parades. She made all our flannel shirts herself: which I hated, as they were itchy to wear.

Abertillery had five cinemas when we were kids. Mam used to talk about seeing Mary Pickford when she was a girl, but we all went to see Pearl White who was in a serial every week. Children went to the pictures on a Saturday morning at half past ten. We would all be given three-halfpence to spend: one penny for the pictures, and then a halfpenny to buy a bruised plum or a damaged apple from the greengrocers. Damaged fruit would be sold off cheap to children. Mam gave us the three-halfpence. Then, later on, when I got a bit older, a silver threepenny bit because I had the responsibility of taking out my crippled sister. She was a sad case. As I was the eldest, it was my responsibility to see she got some fresh air. My little sister Doreen had had polio: it was called meningitis, but she had polio and was paralysed all down one side. It was like a wasting disease. We had a pushchair for her, with a canvas seat. She was put in this, and then out I had to take her. I didn't like it much: but that's why I got more, a silver threepence. Doreen was about three when she got this contagious fever and ended up paralysed.

The school I went to was that of the Church of England in Abertillery. It was a good school and I enjoyed it because I had a good master. If a schoolmaster made a complaint you would get it at home. My father used the strap. We all knew who was boss. If we were out playing and it got to the time when he wanted us all in, he would come to the door and whistle, and then we all knew we had to move— we had to be indoors within a minute. That was the rule.

As boys we did get up to mischief. There were flat drays used for transporting things. The drays had no sides and were pulled by horses. When the men attending the dray reached a steep hill they would harness two extra horses to help pull the load up. Now, when the load was being pulled up, and the men were occupied with the horses, we boys would go behind the dray and make holes in the cardboard boxes piled up there. They might contain apples, plums or pears, and out they would all fall and we could pick them up as they rolled down. The hill was steep and long enough to tilt all the fruit out. There we would be, stuffing the fruit up our jerseys as fast as we could, then make a bolt for it: they wouldn't know what we had. Unfortunately, after a while, they rumbled to us and started to put the fruit at the front of the dray and other goods at the back. The horses were big Clydesdales. At the top of the hill, the two extra trace horses were then unharnessed and sent back to the yard, not very far away. The horses really had to struggle on the cobblestones. We would spend time just watching the horses and the deliveries. Abertillery had a *Bon Marche* and at the side was a big shop frontage with rolls of lino all lined up. After school, we would walk past and push one boy against one and knock the whole lot down: down they would all go all over the place. That amused us.

We boys could also go into Rabiotti's ice-cream parlour (although that sounds a bit grand): we called it the *brachi*. He sold pop, too, and there was a room with a stove it it, we could all sit there, and the boys would spit on the hot stove to see it sizzle. Rabiotti had a one-armed bandit in the room, in the shape of a clown. There were knobs at the side that operated the clown's arm which clutched a cup—the whole point was to try and catch a ball by manipulating the arm. If you succeeded you got a token valued at a penny, or tuppence and the jackpot was fourpence. The token had to be spent in the *brachi* over the counter. We soon learned how to do this without putting any money into the machine. We discovered how to use a hairpin to trigger off the mechanism and have free goes. It was a bit of cheating really.

There seemed to be an Italian or two in each town. They had come to sell ice-cream, and opened up a *brachi*: they were more like a boy's club. Girls didn't hang around in *brachi's*. Italians came to the mining areas and mixed in with us. Rabiotti would go and sell his ice-creams outside the cinema. He would finish about seven o'clock when everybody had gone into the pictures. Then we would help to push his ice-cream cart up the hill back to his shop and get a cornet each for helping.

As well as Italians, there were a lot of Jews around. Our doctor was a Jew, Dr. Simons, a very popular man. His brother was Harry Simons, a boxing promoter: he would treat the young men to drinks. There was a bookie's runner, also a Jew. He would stand on a street corner (no betting shops about in those days) collecting the money. If you got caught betting it was a three shilling fine because the Free Church Congregations had all complained about the gambling that was going on. Another Jew was a glazier—mind, he only put in glass for those that could pay. Jews tended to own property and never worked for anybody else.

In 1922 when I was thirteen, I took the Labour Exam and passed it, so I could leave school and get a job without having to wait until I was fourteen. But I was too young to go down the mine, so I got a job at a greengrocer's and worked a fifty-two hour week. Then, when I was fourteen I got a job at the mine working a forty-eight hour week for 14s.8d, and I got an extra shilling if it was a good week. I was a miner's *butty*, his boy, there to help him, and he was my boss: he paid tuppence a week to the mine doctor to look after me if I got ill, and as I said, an extra shilling bonus if we shifted a lot of coal. We would put vaseline along the lower edge of our eyes so that the coal dust would accumulate there and then we could wipe it off easily.

Down the mine you had to get used to all the mice. They would run across your feet. All your food had to be stored away: the bread and a bit of cheese was kept in a tin, a *tommy*, and a typical prank for boys was to catch a mouse and pop it in the *tommy*, on the sly, and it would be taken home. Usually, it was one of the girls, daughters, well sisters, who opened the *tommy* to clean it out. Out would jump the mouse and she'd be screaming the place down. All our clothes had to be well shaken, a really good shaking to get rid of all the beetles—and the occasional mouse in a pocket—beetles mostly, after every shift. There were thousands of beetles down the mines, especially in the warmer parts. Home we would come, carrying the beetles with us. There were no pit baths then. When we were children we were washed in a zinc bath. But when we were older our baths were taken in half of a thirty-six gallon beer cask: that's what we washed in. You could buy one for half-a-crown. Most miners had one. A woman could wash and do all her dollying in it in the yard. Someone had to keep bringing the boiling water from the kitchen to keep it hot, but you could easily tip it all down the drain at the back door. Our backs were only washed about twice a week, mainly at the weekend, to be clean. There was an old wive's tale that you weakened the back with too much washing. The weekend bath was the big one. As young men we wouldn't go out without our backs washed, after all, if it wasn't clean the black would come through your shirt when you were dancing.

In the Twenties we danced a lot on Saturday nights. One dance we all tried to master was the London Tango: we would dance with a mate until we had mastered it. Then it was time to try it out with a girl—mind, it would be a long time before you danced with a girl. There would be a lot of funny dancing going on as they were all self-taught, trial and error, but we battled on. We would walk to other villages as there was no transport. And we would pay fourpence to get in. The posh one was the Hospital Dance when it came round, at two shillings a ticket—but we didn't have the right clothes for it anyway. We would go to the pictures and see stars like Rudolph Valentino or Ronald Coleman. And we'd want to be like them. Oh! You'd go to a village dance and see Rudolph Valentino types. We would put vaseline on our hair to slick it back. There was a brilliantine, cheap, but if you got hot it would melt and run down all over your forehead, or down your neck. By the time you had done the foxtrot, you'd be hot, and the brilliantine would start to melt.

As for courtship—there was the monkey parade—you started this after a couple of years in a job. You had a bit of money. It was late teens before you had good clothes, the sort needed to join the monkey parade on the main street. There might be four boys and four girls walking up and down after chapel. You would be waiting anxiously for the last hymn to be sung so you could get outside. If a girl accepted you—you *clicked*—off you'd go up the road to the park, or walk along to the next village. It was always walking: that's how you passed the time. Funny enough, you would be walking along with one girl, and pass one you had previously been out with: each one avoiding to look at the other. The majority of girls had a curfew from their parents. Then, when she went home they would ask about the boy, grill her, and then weigh him up. If he was a bit of a rebel that would be the end of it. Everybody knew each other. You were spotted easily. If a girl was going out with a boy the parents didn't like, news got out and there was a lot of gossip. Girls would have to heed what their parents said: she couldn't go against them. Parents didn't want their daughters to go out with coalminers: but that was ninety percent of us. There was snobbery about. Parents wanted girls to go out with young men working in shops, or a manager's son. Girls who had had singing lessons, or who played the piano, were all thought of as superior beings, with a chance to marry someone better than a miner.

I was seventeen when the General Strike hit us in 1926: all the mines were closed down. Dad wasn't allowed any dole because he was on strike. Mam was on the parish, poor relief, and got a blue chit, worth about five shillings according to the size of the family: it was for the women and children only and did not cover the men. There was still the rent which had to be paid eventually—it mounted up—all the women were worried to death about the rent and paying their way. Mam got a bit of help from our grandparents, and her brothers were not miners, so they could chip in and help too. But Mam *was* sometimes in debt with the rent. But then, she was never out of debt really, all the time, until the children got bigger and brought in some money.

It was during the General Strike that me and my mates went to the soup kitchen. Of a morning it would open up about 8.30am. to feed us a breakfast. It was located in the Baptist Chapel. We would be given bread and margarine and marmalade. At home we generally had treacle on our bread for breakfast, so this was the first time I had had marmalade: it was a novelty. Going out to this place of a morning, out with the other boys (we were all about seventeen or so) was fun. We all looked forward to it. It used up time when there was nothing to do. Mind, people tried to keep their spirits up by making entertainments out in the street. Once someone brought out a piano, into the street, and started to play dance tunes: there were two boys dancing with hobnailed boots on.

At mid-day we went back to the Baptist Chapel to be dished up our dinner. They supplied us with basins and spoons and served up corned beef stew—that was on the menu regularly—bread, and a mug of tea. It was all run by women volunteers, lady members of the chapel would come and serve. The Chairman of the Council's daughter came as a volunteer: she would help to give out the food. Then, in the afternoon, there was bread and margarine and a slabcake, with tea. We all enjoyed it. It *occupied* us, you see. There was nothing else to do. And it was sociable. Saturday and Sunday there were no free meals and you had to rely on your own family. So on Saturday it was only bread and dripping for dinner: not much else. Not as good as the soup kitchen. Mam would try her hardest to give us a Sunday dinner: but there was more variety at the welfare meals. That's why we liked going. We did quite well in Abertillery.

The General Strike in Wales lasted from May of 1926 until December. As the mine owners had not allowed any maintenance work to be done the mines were all in a terrible condition. So, when we went back to work only half of us could be employed as it was so dangerous in parts of the mines. A lot of the older men were victimised because they were connected with the union.

It took me weeks and weeks to find work. In the coal mine there are different districts. I would go to the overman of the area and ask if he knew of any man who wanted a boy: a *butty*. You remained a *butty* from thirteen until you were twenty-one then they found you a journeyman's job. Most miners wanted as young a *butty* as possible because they got less wages. The older you got, the more they had to give you. By the time you were twenty-one you got £2.8s.0d. But when you started at fourteen it was 14s.8d. a week for forty-eight hours, six days a week. Being seventeen, naturally I was going to be more expensive than a fourteen year-old *butty*. As hard as I tried, there was nothing for me. No work. Nothing available for me down the mine. It was a hard time.

On the dole I went, with 15s.3d. a week, but they came round and means tested us before they let me have it. People hated the means test. It was terrible. They would come round, these officials, and look at the furniture, the chairs. They would say some of it *had* to be sold. Some people would have an organ in their front parlour. If you were forced onto the dole, the means test people would come round, look in all the rooms and tell you to sell the organ first, anything of value had to go. It had to be sold.

I got so demoralized on the dole. There was nothing to do. So I thought that I would leave Wales, and find employment elsewhere. There was some short time in the mines, but nothing much. So, in 1930 (that's when I was twenty odd) I went off to Stratford-upon-Avon as boots under the porter at the White Swan.

At the White Swan I got paid twelve shillings a week, plus food, and averaged about seven shillings a week in tips, so the money was quite good. I could even send a 2s.6d. postal order home to Mam every week to help her out. My sisters were still at school and living at home, so she needed the money. At Christmas time I sent home a five shilling postal order. The proprietors wife was Welsh at the hotel, so they were friendly to me.

I stayed about a year and a half at the White Swan but then they were taken over and wanted more experienced people. So back home to Abertillery I went: no work there. Eventually I found a job working in the kitchen of a big nursing home in Boscombe, near Bournemouth. There I got twenty-nine shillings a week and my keep, so I took out a Post Office book. By then my sisters had left school and were working, and so was Dad. I vowed that I never wanted to be without a shilling any more and so started my savings. From the nursing home kitchen I went to work on the Wembley Swimming Pool as a labourer. These were all short-term jobs but they saved me from being demoralized: they were jobs. I learned a lot about life, and about things as I moved around. When the Wembley job finished I went back home again, but there were no jobs in Wales. My mates, and me, we all got fed up and so went on a training scheme that had been set up, to train young men as plumbers. There was six month's training at Park Royal, near Wembley, but afterwards—no jobs: the same old story. A little bit later, though, the pits *were* opening up again (around 1937) with the advent of war. There were jobs in the mines again. So after all that travelling around, and the training scheme, it was back down the mine for me, until after the war was over.

ALYS GRENFELL OF BRYNHYFRYD, SWANSEA

Born February 17th, 1912
Daughter of Ernest Grenfell and his wife
Alice Grenfell née Taylor

Our Ma was just sixteen when she first met Pa: it would have been in 1897. Her parents were staunch Wesleyan Methodists from Bideford, attending the English speaking chapel at Landore. Ma was a young Sunday School teacher and that's how they met, as Pa, too, taught Sunday School. There was some opposition at first, from her parents, as Pa was nearly twenty-one, but they were able to see each other regularly at chapel events, and we still have all the love letters they wrote to each other over the years of their courtship. The one he wrote on January 31st, 1898 shows us his feelings on his birthday:

As I could not sleep last night I took up *Somebody's Luggage* and finished reading it. I think it very similar to a part of *Stepping Heavenward* only in one case it's the young man that is not worthy and in the other the young woman. I hope there is no leak in our boat like there was in theirs, we have both sailed the waters of love before but there has been a leak in the boat, I do hope there is no leak in ours. But I'm going right away from what I intended to tell you, you asked me a fair question and the least I could have done was to answer it. I refrained from doing so because I am so much older than you are, and never liked anyone to know my age. I ask your forgiveness for not answering you last night. I could not rest untill (sic) I had told you, so I write today to tell you that this is my 21st birthday, hoping my age makes no difference to you.

Ma answered it immediately, as her letter is also dated the 31st of January. Postal delivery must have been the same day in those days.

Really, your letter surprised me this evening. If you have cause to ask to be forgiven by me, how much more so, do I need forgiveness from you. Oh, Ernie, if I have been the means of making your cross

102

harder to bear, do forgive me, I would not wish, by any means, to stand in your light, so please will you let me know. I have felt very unhappy since last night, because I did not know the reason why you would not let me know your age. I did guess that it was your 21st birthday today, but I wanted you to tell me out straight. I will not be 17 until March so you can guess the difference which there is between us. It said in your letter you hoped your age would not make any difference to me, God forbid, that I should be the means in making the difference, although I am much younger than you, I trust that God will fill me with Divine love, and that my love for you will be made stronger and purer.

The age difference was only four years really. I can understand Pa's attraction to her. She was lovely. Strawberry blond hair, very blue eyes, and a lovely complexion. And she came from a highly respected family—her father, James Taylor, was a well-known builder and contractor in the neighbourhood and his wife kept a shop and was the local midwife. Ma Taylor was highly thought of by everyone and Grandpa Taylor's houses had a reputation for being well-built. People buying a house in the district would be happy if they were told that he had built it. And, of course, they were staunchly teetotal: drink was never taken into their home. They were both dead against it. Our Ma had been brought up to despise drink as the road to ruin. And it *was* for so many families. Our Pa had his own experience of this.

Pa had had his childhood spoiled by the fact that both his parents liked drink. He was a victim of circumstances. As children we were all brought up to strongly oppose the taking of alcohol. Pa had taken the pledge when he was a boy, not to touch it. He saw what it had done to his own parents. In many ways his life was sad. He was highly intelligent, gifted, and very religious, and he hated having to work at Cwmfelin Steel Works: it almost destroyed him. The Grenfell family make an interesting study.

We were all brought up knowing that we were the same family as Sir Richard Grenville of the *Revenge*, the English Admiral who had fought the Spanish Fleet off the Azores in the time of Queen Elizabeth I. Lord Tennyson had written a famous poem about him. Although we spelled our name Grenfell, we were Grenvilles, and Pa made sure we all knew who our ancestors were. The Grenvilles were Lords of the Manor of Bideford, High Sheriffs of Cornwall for generations: and one of the biggest landowners there. Once our Pa met Field Marshall Lord Grenfell of Kilvey, one of the aristocratic Grenfells, and he acknowledged Pa as a relation. Lord Grenfell's family and ours came from St. Just. They both had this *thing* about being of Norman descent. You could call it ancestor worship, but all the Grenfells knew their roots. Our great-grandfather, William Grenfell, came to Swansea from Cornwall in the 1850s when he was appointed Agent of Morfa Copper Works. His brother, Thomas Shugge Grenfell had already come to Swansea to live and work as an accountant. A lot of Cornish people were coming to Swansea as it was a boom town. The story in the family is that our great-grandfather, William Grenfell, invested all his money in a venture to manufacture a metal that looked exactly like gold. He had a gentleman's agreement with a friend, to produce this metal: but the friend swindled him out of the profits and he lost all his money. That's the story. Our grandfather, Richard Grenfell, had been well-educated, privately, and was sent to be apprenticed as a pattern-maker, which is a highly skilled draughtsman's job—a profession—and he married Eliza Glover, the daughter of Thomas Glover, a cabinet maker with shop premises on Oxford Street (his wife, Maria had her own antique shop and was a noted antiquarian in Swansea. She was the daughter of Councillor George Osborne Whittaker of Bideford). Everything should have been fine. But Eliza liked to drink. They *both* did. That was their failing. Money which should have gone into the education of their children was spent on alcohol. Instead of seeing that his salary paid for opportunities for their children, it was squandered. One of the letters our Pa wrote to Ma is all about the excitement of his mother deciding to give up drink. It is dated May 9th, 1899.

Now *Dearest* I am going to make a request, I want you to do something for your Ernie. My mother has signed the pledge and I want you to pray that she may have grace to always keep it. You must think how delighted I am because it is a step in the right direction.

Unfortunately it didn't last very long. But Ma wasn't to know this, and so she wrote back enthusiastically the following day.

It is with gentle and loving thoughts, I answer your letter. Dearest Ernie you must feel very happy, now your mother has signed the pledge. I felt like shouting, praise God when I read your letter. What an encouragement it is for us, to pray and trust on. You want me to pray that the Lord will help her to keep it. Dearest Ernie you know I will. Think what it will mean to you, and I do try, to do all I can, to make you happier, whether I fail to do so, I can't say. I'll tell you now dear Ernie, that many a time, when I have been praying for your mother, I have risen from my knees with my face wet with tears, and also with confidence in God that He would answer our prayers. We read in God's word, that he who soweth in tears, shall reap with joy. It is quite true because this is a true proof of it.

She writes with all the enthusiasm of an eighteen-year-old. Ma knew that her own home was so unlike that of Pa's. Her mother was a staunch member of the British Women's Temperance Association. Alcohol was taboo. Our Pa must have constantly been thinking how nice it would be to have his own home. It was a pity Ma was still too young to leave her family. As one of the elder daughters (and her mother was to have fourteen children) she was needed in the house to help her own mother with the work. But we can tell marriage was on his mind. On May 11th 1899 he wrote again.

You say *Dearest* that I must have felt warm hearted when I wrote my last letter, well, yes I do get heated sometimes and you should not wonder at it when you know what a dear noble little woman I have got to love, now do not say I am flattering because I'm not, I mean every word of it. I would dearly like to be off today so that I could enjoy your company, but as I can't I hope that you will have a good time. You can be sure Alice Dear that I will be down at eight on Saturday and bring the parcel too I could not miss any chance of seeing you. I have been reading such a beautiful tale this week, one of Sheldon's about a young man and young woman who were married and went away to a mission to work for their Master. They were so very happy although they were very poor. Theirs were such lives of self sacrifice that I thought how nice it would be for you and I to work together like they did. They had many troubles like you and I may have, but Christ was always there to bless them and He made them rich at last. And we are rich too *Dearest* for have we not found the pearl of greatest price . . .

Although they only lived a mile and a half or so apart, they constantly wrote letters to each other. Their courtship was played out with chapel life serving as a means of communication. There were prayer meetings and services. Ma was very much kept at home by her parents. They didn't want her to marry at such a young age. Yet they were so much in love. It must have been a strain on them. At some point they became formally engaged as Ma had a very nice engagement ring with three diamonds set like stars in a wide gold band. The very last but one letter (and we have fifty-five of them) shows Pa's main concern at this time. It was written on July 18th 1900.

Dearest Alice in your letter you express a wish that is the main feature in my life. It is my greatest longing to be able to make a home of our own, and I know that it will be the happiest in the whole world, because you are so good and thoughtful that it can be none other. I am sure Dearest we are both doing and will do all that we possibly can to make our home all that a home could be. I hope the time is not far off. Before I close I must tell you that the information contained in your letter will help me considerably . . . Your Ever loving Ernie.

We don't know what that information was, Ma's letter is missing. We do know that she became pregnant. Perhaps they both wanted to force Ma's parents to let them marry. It must have caused pandemonium when Ma's parents found out she was going to have a baby. Her mother was very staid. But they had been courting for a number of years, and Pa was anxious to set up a home for himself.

Ma was nineteen and married in pale green (she must have looked lovely with her strawberry blond hair): it would be a pastel shade, not white—not in those days and Grandma Taylor was a stickler for the conventions. Ma couldn't have married in white when she was five months pregnant. It was in the autumn of 1900. She never ever discussed her wedding. Although we did know that a pot of blue campanula which grew in the conservatory was grown from a bit of her bridal bouquet. Years later, it came out that she was pregnant before she married and she was furious: it was such a shock to us. She was so prim and proper. Ruth was born in April 1901.

Once she had told her parents about her pregnancy they stood by her. After the wedding Ma and Pa went into rooms on the same street where she lived. This was temporary accommodation whilst Ma's father prepared a house for them. While they were in lodgings Grandpa Taylor added two more rooms to the house next door to his, and put up quite a high garden wall. Apart from Ma's parent's house, which was a big corner house, four bedroomed at the end of the street, all the others were mostly two bedroomed with open gardens. So Ma's father added this high garden wall, too high to lookover, so Ma had her privacy. She was adamant about privacy and would not let the neighbours have a view into *her* garden. Grandpa Taylor saw to it that she had an extra bedroom and a new bigger kitchen. When all this was ready, then they moved in, renting the house from her father, who owned it.

By the time she was thirty, Ma had given birth to seven children (and her hair had turned a deep nut-brown). There were no miscarriages or infant deaths. Ruth was the first in 1901; then Clifford in 1902; Irene in 1903; John in 1906; Ronald in 1910 and Mabel and me in 1912—the twins.

My mother didn't know that she was going to have twins. She went into labour, and gave birth to my sister Mabel. She was a big baby. The midwife cleared up everything, but a little while later my mother went into labour again, and everybody was surprised. I was so tiny the midwife didn't think much of my chances and popped me into a little half-pint jug which was on the dressing-table. My Ma wouldn't have that, she wasn't going to lose me; she made them save me, but I don't think that they were keen. After all, I was the seventh child; probably they thought one more or less didn't really matter. Although such things were never *ever* mentioned (and I don't know how they managed it), but there were no more children. I'm sure Ma felt that she had done her duty. Six pregnancies in twelve years of marriage is enough for any woman. She probably was adamant about not repeating her own mother's total of fourteen—and the last one born when Grandma Taylor was fifty-four in 1909—called Phyllis—they were lucky because she was able to nurse them in their old age.

Our Ma was a good mother, really good. Caring. And always ready to do a good turn when it was needed. When our cousin Roy fell through a glasshouse and got covered in splinters, it was our Ma who sat up all night at the hospital picking out all the glass splinters with a tweezers, hours it took her, and she saying: 'I'm not going to let a boy like this go, he's *not* going to die, he's *not.*' And she did it. Covered in glass splinters he was from head to toe. And the only child her brother had. But she got him through. She was always kind to us and others. Ma was a generous woman. She lived by her Christian convictions.

Ma was a strong willed woman. The manager of the household. Really it would have been better if she had been given a profession. Her intelligence was wasted. We always felt that she would have been a happier woman, more fulfilled, if she could have run a business of some kind. She must have been frustrated, and perhaps even resentful that some of her younger sisters were allowed specific training: one was a teacher, another a nurse. But Ma, being one of the older girls was expected to stay at home and help *her* Ma run the house. This made her all the more determined that her daughters would be given opportunities to develop their own particular talents.

Pa was a great believer in the science of phrenology: that the shape of the head was the key to our nature. In the Mackworth Arcade in Swansea, was a phrenologist, so we were all taken there to have our heads read at the appropriate age. The phrenologist placed his hands on your head and felt the shape of it, and all the bumps: from these he could tell your nature and what you would be good at. Pa so believed in the truth of this science, that he stuck by what the phrenologist said, and had all of us trained up as suggested. Ruth was told she would make a fine teacher, and so eventually she was sent to a teachers' training college; John was thought to be clerical and so went into an office; Irene had a creative gift and so it was suggested that she would make a good milliner; Clifford was told he would make a talented artist and so went to art school; Ronald he thought was a practical type who would be happiest as a carpenter, so he was sent as an apprentice. Mabel was also told she would make an excellent office worker and so was sent to Clark's Secretarial College. As for me, well, when the phrenologist felt my bumps he said that I was highly artistic and creative, but my temperament was unsuited for the work-force: that I was too nervous and highly strung to cope with being out at work. So although they sent me to Swansea College of Art to learn design and dressmaking, I never went out to work. I stayed at home with them until I married at twenty-five.

Ruth was my eldest sister, a beautiful girl: we all loved her for her sweet nature. She was the cleverest of us all, but when she applied to the teachers' training college they turned her down; didn't offer her a place. Ma was astounded. Now this shows how determined she could be. She would *not* accept the refusal and so went to see the principal herself. Ma could be very persuasive. When she was dressed to go out, and with *her* looks, well, she was lovely. The principal changed his mind, and Ruth became a teacher. After her training, she found a job in Gilfach Goch, in the Rhondda, teaching the children of miners. It was there that she became engaged after a while. It created quite a stir at home. Remember, I was only a small girl, and private matters were never discussed in front of us as Ma thought it improper. All I know is that Ruth was forced to break off the engagement: they would *not* have it. The man was a miner. Whether it was that which bothered them I don't know. Or it might have been the fact that married women could not teach in the 1920s: as soon as they married they had to leave the profession. Well, Ruth was newly trained. Our parents had spent a lot of money educating her to be a teacher, and all this would be thrown away if she married. Shortly after breaking off her engagement she found a job at Dyfatty School in Swansea and came back home to live with us. Poor Ruth, she never did marry but lived with Ma and Pa until she died in 1956, a spinster. It shows the power parents could have over their daughters. Even in the 1920s girls had to be dutiful.

It is possible that Mabel and I went to school at three and a half, certainly four. If the families were large, they would let them in when they were three and a half. I enjoyed school: I liked art and needlework best. Most of the girls wore calico pinafores over their dresses and lace-up boots. We had a Penny Bank at school, and children took in a sum of money each week. It helped their mothers save a bit. The interest which had been earned during the year was spent on a bag of sweets at Christmas for each child, plus an orange and an apple. At Easter the accumulated interest would be spent on four little sugar Easter eggs for each of us.

Sometimes, at Brynhyfryd School, during playtime, the teachers would join in and play with us—it could be a chain game during which we would form a line holding waists and going around the school yard. This we would do in cold weather to keep ourselves warm. The teachers enjoyed it as well, and we'd all be laughing. Then there was a game called *Oranges and Lemons*, which comprised two players facing each other, they would clasp hands and the rest would run around and under our outstretched hands. We would all be singing 'Oranges and a lemon' and after so many had passed we would suddenly stop, and *that* child would be asked whether they wanted to be an orange or a lemon. This was a great decision as one teacher would be an orange and the other a lemon. At the end of the game heads would be counted, and the teacher with the most children would be the winner.

The atmosphere was good in school. There were school dinners for the poorer classes to have. And every morning we were given half-a-pint of milk to drink at break-time. On May Day the teachers would have a Maypole put up and we would be taught to dance around it holding different coloured ribbons. It was quite complicated. St. David's Day was also another big event, with some girls dressing up in Welsh costumes: not all of them did this. In our craft lessons we were taught how to hem squares of calico. And we had basket-weaving with raffia. It was the sewing that I liked the best. At home Ma would embroider a lot in the evenings, and also crochet trimmings for sheets and tablecloths. Every pillowcase was trimmed with crochet. At home my evenings would also be spent in doing needlework as we were not allowed out in the later part of the evening because drink was cheap and it was not wise for us to stay out too late. My Auntie Kate taught me to knit before I even went to school. There would be a penny ball of rainbow wool one could buy at Nanny Gonaways, and I'd sit on the staircase and knit squares, or things for my dolls. The first thing I ever knitted was a peacock blue jumper for a doll in garter stitch: that's the stitch I started off with. Ma saw to it that we girls could all embroider, knit and crochet. As a young girl Ma had been sent over to Bideford to live with her Auntie Kate, expressly to be taught how to make collars and cuffs. This particular aunt was a tailoress, and as it was expected that a wife would make her family's clothes, the making of professional looking collars and cuffs was important if the children's clothes were to look good. Ma had a sewing machine. Her needlework was amazing: she could do the finest stitching and her mending of a hole was almost invisible. As I have said, Ruth was the academic one, it was our other older sister Irene, who was apprenticed to a milliner and dressmaker.

Nine years older than us, Irene was apprenticed to a Mrs. Howells of Treboeth. Later, Ma gave her a room at home to work from: her customers were acquired by word of mouth and she had plenty of work. She could also make clothes for the family. She made all of Ma's hats. Once Irene made us green velvet dresses, and my twin sister and I had to wear our pinafores over them on Sundays, the day we wore them. Ma always trimmed our best pinafores with *broiderie-anglaise*: the ones we wore for school were calico as well, but without trimmings.

We all went to the Wesleyan Methodists Chapel at Landore: three times on a Sunday. Our grandparents Taylor would also be there as well. And other Devonian families. At Band of Hope we would all wear our temperance badges after taking the pledge *never* to touch alcohol. Each night when we were put to bed we had to kneel down beside the bed and say our prayers before Ma went downstairs. There were so many of us in the family that each child was allowed to bring a friend home for tea on Sunday, and each one of us would take it in turn until we had all entertained a friend. At 6.30pm. we would all go back to chapel for an hour. Our parents allowed no playing in the street on Sunday, or unruly games: it was kept quietly, as the Sabbath. We could sit and read, whatever we pleased, but certainly never play outside: *that* was an iron rule. We liked going to chapel. And to Band of Hope: it was a nice evening out for us.

The Sunday School outing was very important to us. It was on Whit Monday I seem to remember. The chapel would hire a canal barge drawn by horses to take us all along the Landore canal to a park. If it was wet the schoolroom of the Church was rented for the tea. But if it was fine the tea was taken outdoors. There might be two canal boats, and chapel volunteers went to the canal on the Saturday to clean and deck them up with calico and other trimmings ready for the Monday. Sometimes the destination was Clydach. Long tables would be put out and we all ate bread and butter, followed by cherry cake and fruit cake and tea: it wasn't much, but some of the poorer children thought it wonderful. There were games and prizes: a sack race, a three-legged race, an egg race. It was worth going to Sunday School to be part of it. Then we had a prize-giving day once a year in chapel: the better attendances to Sunday School got the better book.

Our father read his Bible daily. He also liked to spend his leisure hours doing fretwork—that is whenever he wasn't engaged in chapel work—however, there was a great deal of trouble when we twins were about ten or eleven: 1923 or so. There was a big bust up at our chapel and Pa left to join the Jehovah Witnesses. This was a terrible time for our Ma. She did not approve of Jehovah Witnesses and refused to join them. The atmosphere at home changed as a result. Pa would have Sunday dinner with us all, and then leave straightaway and not come back until the evening. Ma continued to refuse to have anything to do with the Jehovah Witnesses, preferring the Wesleyan Methodists. This was really the start of their drifting apart as Ma stopped going to chapel on her own. She wanted us to worship as a family. Pa was stubborn about it. In the end he didn't find religious satisfaction with the Jehovah Witnesses either, and stopped going. In the end he just read his Bible at home, alone. Then only we children went to chapel. Politics were never discussed.

The week prior to Palm Sunday all the women would take down their curtains, and those who could afford a summer set put up fresh curtains ready for Palm Sunday. Our Ma's windows were always greatly admired as she always put up a new set for the summer months. No-one wanted dirty looking curtains to be noticed by all the people passing with bunches of flowers for the graves. Palm Sunday was important for visiting the cemetery. This ritual of changing the curtains also included the carpets and rugs which all had to be taken up and beaten clean, so everything was fresh looking. We twins would go with Pa on Palm Sunday morning to put flowers on the family graves. Ma would have the winter curtains washed and put away until October, when they were brought out and put up in each of the rooms. Every window was changed: eight windows in all when we lived at *Sheridan*.

The curtains seem very important. Ma never gossiped, never mixed with other women in the neighbourhood, our lives were private. No-one could see in. There were fine lace ruched curtains on rods right against the window frame, then full-length heavier lace curtains hanging from an inner rail at the top, and on top again figured velvet curtains completely blocked out the street. Ma couldn't see out and no-one could see in. It reduced the light too, made the rooms very dark. The drapes for the summer months, the curtains, were a lighter crettone, but it still prevented people from seeing in. Ma only mixed with other members of our chapel, and the friends we were allowed to ask to tea, were our chapel friends. She never just 'went out', out for no purpose. It was usually only to go to a chapel service or meeting. Ma valued her privacy. She thought it improper for us to be peering outside, moving the curtains, and to be seen looking out of the bedroom windows, well, that was terrible. A woman daren't be seen with her face in the window of an upstairs room. Shocking.

Ma was always reserved in her behaviour. No loud laughing, joking, nothing like that. Conversation was modest. There were many things not thought proper for discussion, one of them being pregnancy. She behaved as a lady should. Manners were very important to her. She was very proper. As a child and young girl I just wasn't aware of pregnancy: it never crossed my mind. It didn't seem something that we noticed—women having babies—perhaps it was because they hid it so well. They probably did want to conceal it as best they could. Being pregnant was a very private thing. Of course, we knew nothing about sex. We didn't even know the word. When we girls started to menstruate it was a mystery. Nothing was ever explained to us. We girls did not know why we were bleeding: it just happened. I did not know why it was happening until after I married at twenty-five, and then it was my husband who explained its function (I think the men then knew more about it than the women. Boys know more. They talk about it more). When we were menstruating our mother cut up pieces of old sheets which she hemmed, so that they could be washed and used again. On wash-day they were left soaking in a tub of salt water and then Ma's washer-woman put them into the copper at the end of the wash.

Monday was wash day. Each Monday morning it was my job to get up early and go down the garden to the wash-house. There I would have to fill the copper with gallons of water: that would take ages. Then I had to light a fire under it of sticks and coal. The water had to be boiling before my mother's washer-woman came at nine o'clock. She always wore a big Welsh shawl and a man's cloth cap. Perhaps I'd get up two hours before school to get it done. I never minded this job and liked to do it. The washer-woman's name was Mrs. Matthews and she stayed until 3.30pm. and she would get 3s.6d. for this (that's the sum I seem to remember), because she was washing for a family of nine. My mother would give her a hot dinner mid-day, which she would look forward to. There was no mangle for Mrs. Matthews: she had a hard scrubbing-board, and the poor thing had to wring everything out by hand. On wet days all the washing had to be hung up inside the wash-house.

The ironing was done over a couple of days. There was an iron shelf which hooked onto the bars of the fire, with the irons standing up with the flat of the iron catching the heat. You had to try the heat on a piece of newspaper: if it didn't scorch it, it was O.K. to use. Ma would do some ironing, then all we girls had to chip in. The older girls had to darn and patch anything which needed doing. Ma was a stickler for mending things.

The house was run on very strict, well-ordered lines. Ma made *no* distinction between the boys and we girls. There were regular jobs for all of us to do: all shared out. My two brothers Ronald and Clifford had to scrub all the vegetables clean before Ma would prepare them: she would *not* touch a potato to peel it until it was clean. John would have to pod the peas or runner beans ready to cook. As John was the

eldest boy he did all the shopping in town, in Swansea. There was a
tram that went from Brynhyfryd to the *Maypole*: that's where Ma sent
him: she never went herself. It was also John's job to fill the coal
buckets in the morning before school, and bring them into the house
ready for Ma to keep the fire going—and he had to do the same again
when he came home from school. It was Pa who always got the
kitchen fire prepared and going before he left for work in the morning.
Sister Rene had to get our mother's breakfast ready and take it up to
her on a tray to have in bed. Ma *never* got up to give us breakfast: we all
had to forage for ourselves. After Rene had taken up the breakfast tray
she had to freestone the front step before going to school. Our eldest
sister Ruth had to make up the boys beds, and empty all the chamber
pots as there was no indoor lavatory at number 25 Freeman Street. But
we did have one later when we moved next-door into our
grandparent's house. It was a real hive of activity in the morning. I used
to have to black-lead the fireplaces: the bars would be reddish after the
fire the day before: I had to black-lead all of them before going to
school. The fire-bars had to be kept black each day. Once a week all
the brass had to be cleaned: fenders and tongs. We had to twist up the
newspapers for fire-lighting, and also cut them up into squares so that
they could be strung up and put out in the lavatory.

Saturdays were spent getting the house looking clean and orderly for
Sunday. As Clifford got older he used to find it a bit trying to have to
do all his chores: there was so much brass—even the stair rods were
brass—and he had to clean them. He had to take up the mats, and put
them outside on the line, then go in and sweep the floors. In a lot of
houses there were flagstones, usually sprinkled with fine sand. But we
had a number of mats spread about: even in the kitchen. Ma made her
own bread (like most women) and one of us had to take it to the local
bakehouse at dinner-time and call back for it at night. We had to see
that it had a special fork mark on it to be sure that it was ours. Our
brothers did not have part-time jobs before they left school.

As we lived next door to Ma's parents we saw a lot of them. Our
Grandma Taylor was well-known in the neighbourhood: when women
wanted a capable and clean midwife, they sent for *her*. She loved her
temperance teas at chapel. She had a special teapot for them, with

Wesley on one side, and the doxology on the other. That, and a big tray of cakes had to be got ready to be taken down. Grandma Taylor was an amazing woman. She was an avid reader and her eyesight never deteriorated. She *never* had glasses, never needed them, and yet she read right up until she died at eighty-nine. Occasionally I would visit and read Grandpa Taylor the Bible: he would have nothing else read to him. Really he was a disappointed man. Our grandfather had built for himself a lovely house at the top of our street, but never moved in. When war came in 1914 he went bankrupt. The building trade just came to a halt. He wasn't able to build any more houses. He was also owed a great deal of money. And, I believe, was never repaid. It was Grandpa's nature was the ruin of him: too kind to *force* payment for bills owed him. He would never take anyone to court for debt. After the war there was unemployment and things did not improve. In the end he had a nervous breakdown and was taken away to recover. Eventually it was decided to sell the property they had. At the time it consisted of two houses (one with a corner shop), stabling and workshops. Our Ma was determined to buy it all. At the same time there was another property with a shop at the front, halfway up the street, with quite a lot of land behind it. This property Pa wanted to buy so that he could cultivate it and sell the produce, but no, Ma wouldn't have it. It had to be *her* parent's property. And, of course, she got her own way. You could call her a determined woman. When she had a plan, it was followed through. Money was borrowed from the *Rechabites*[1] and from Auntie Kate (she was our Ma's sister and lived near us) and our grandparent's property bought. When we moved into their old house, the shop at the front was rented out, as were the stables and workshops: this brought in a regular income which Ma controlled: she was the manager. The new house had a conservatory entrance, quite a sizeable one, and Ma could keep a scales in there, and sell some of the produce Pa grew on his allotment. All this helped to pay off the loans.

We always had wonderful Christmases. Ma would make her own mincemeat, Christmas puddings and cakes. Paper garlands and Japanese

[1] The Independent Order of Rechabites, the biggest of the temperance friendly societies, had been named after a water-drinking tribe in the Old Testament. Founded in 1835, by 1890 it had 142,000 members.

lanterns would decorate the house. We always put our stockings up hanging from the mantelpiece. The stockings would be filled with nuts and fruits, sweets and knick-knacks. Then there would be our annual books, and always a doll each for the girls. We always had a turkey dinner. No alcohol allowed, of course, just Pa's home-made ginger wine, which was served in a very dainty glass decanter. Visitors at Christmas time were always given ginger wine to drink. On Christmas day evening we would have a cold meal, with lots of relations calling.

We saw a lot of relatives. And only mixed with other Devonian or Cornish families: those whose grandparents or parents had come over to Swansea in the last century. The Welsh went to their own chapels. We didn't think of ourselves as Welsh at all, although our parents had been born in Wales. We had separate identities from those who were Welsh. The Taylors kept in touch with their relatives in Bideford, and our grandparents spent holidays with the ones who had farms: one of Grandma Taylor's brothers had a big farm at Chumleigh. The Grenfells were even out in America. Our Uncle Bowen, for example, had been leading an Evangelical Preaching Mission to San Fransisco when the earthquake struck in 1903. He was there. Thinking of the Grenfells— Grandma Grenfell could not abide vehicles or anything motorised. She refused ever to travel by tram-car, and there was a good tram-car service from Cwmbwrla (near where she lived in Manselton) into Swansea. But, no, she didn't like them. She never travelled in anything with an engine. I suppose when she was young she had ridden in a pony and trap, or cab. When I married in 1937, she refused to come to the wedding in a taxi and walked instead. Really, she was marvellous. She walked everywhere and seemed to have abundant energy even in her eighties.

Our childhood was happy. We went to the cinema on a Saturday afternoon for the matinee performance. We had to walk all the way into town—a couple of miles—and Pa would come with us. Ma hardly ever went: it was not her scene. But Pa loved going, and especially liked Shirley Temple: he wouldn't miss a film with *her* in it. Dick Powell films we loved because there was always a little dog in them.

When we were about ten or eleven Mabel and I started to go to the Baths at Morriston: cutting through Llewellyn's Park to get there. We had to walk the whole way, quite a few miles. Just once a week we went, and paid tuppence to go in. At thirteen I dived in, and hit my head on a pipe, which cut my head open. The people saw the blood in the water and called the attendant. I was taken to Cousin Winnie Andrewartha's who lived just nearby: she took me to her doctor who gave me two stitches. They all said I was lucky to survive. Auntie Edie came each morning to bathe my head and put a dressing on. She was one of Ma's younger sisters and had trained as a nurse. The sisters always rallied round when one needed help.

My sister and I left school at fourteen. I had to stay at home to help Ma with the housework, whilst Mabel went to Clark's College to learn shorthand and typing. After all, the phrenologist had said she would be good at clerical work. At sixteen it was decided that Mabel would go to find employment in London. She was not happy about this, but in the late 20s there were so few opportunities for girls who were typists in south Wales. Mabel had the training, and so it was decided that she would leave home in order to relieve the pressure on the family. She was very resentful and unhappy about this, but Ma arranged for her to go and live with her cousin who had a house in London: off she went and never lived at home again.

For the first few years after school, I stayed at home, but eventually it was decided to send me to the Art College: it was there that I fell in love. One day I walked into the entrance hall, looked up the stairs, and there at the top was a young man, staring down at me. I thought 'He's handsome.' It was love at first sight. Ernie had this lovely colouring, and yellow-green eyes. We started our courting, meeting at Art College, and walking miles out together. Eventually when we got engaged, we bought a tandem so we could go riding together. It was wonderful. Such freedom. The whole of Gower to explore. But we were *forbidden* by my parents to go cycling on a Sunday. Ernie was supposed to accompany me to the Congregational Church in Manselton. By the time we were in our twenties we thought this a bit unreasonable, but we dare not go against Ma and Pa's wishes. So on a Sunday morning I would dress up in my best clothes, say I was having lunch at Ernie's, but go there and change into my cycling clothes and off we would go: perhaps off to Oxwich Bay with a picnic lunch. It was wonderful cycling along together. Then in the evening, I would put my church clothes back on again, and Ernie would wear his Sunday suit and take me back home and we would pretend we had been in church for morning and evening services. It was *very* wicked of us really: we shouldn't have done it.

JESSIE HARVEY OF SWANSEA
Born October 10th, 1912

I was one of a family of seven children and the eldest of four girls when my mother died of influenza in February 1922. I was nine years old. It was decided that we girls should remain together, and with the help of our school governess[1] (Infants) we were placed in the Swansea Orphan Home for Girls. It housed about fifty inmates. Parent or guardians were expected to pay a small sum weekly, but I'm afraid for many of us that did not last long.

My memories of our entry to the home, strangely enough, are quite vague. I do remember some anxiety about my sisters that all would be well with them. Fear did not enter into it, for the staff attending us were very kind, but I really could not imagine home without my mother. My youngest sister, eighteen months old, arrived at a later date to the joy of Matron who adored babies. She was the first baby to be admitted and was treated like a princess, loved by all the staff. We had very little to do with her at that stage. In fact, our way of life rather divided us all. We lived according to our ages, in the dining room, dormitories and school, of course.

We sat at long tables on forms for our meals, with a member of the staff on duty eating her meal at a small table. Breakfast was a round of bread and margarine and porridge or bread and milk and tea. Dinners were mainly soup and rice pudding or sometimes bread pudding. On Sunday, something more meaty like cottage pie and a suet pudding; Roly Poly as we called it. Tea, again, was a round of bread and margarine and tea, but on Saturday jam, and lettuce in the Summer. Seedcake on Sunday, which I happily exchanged for bread. I did not like seedcake. That was our last meal of the day. We did have extras in the Summer, for example, strawberries and greengages given to us by kind friends. Talking at meals was *not* permitted and we were punished if we disobeyed.

We slept in large, airy dormitories, varying in size. We each had our own bed, which we made every morning under supervision. The beds were wholesome. A hessian over the springs, mattress cover, under

[1] A headmistress was often called the 'governess' at this time.

blanket, sheets, one pillow and over the white blankets a red one, which gave the dormitories a warm, cheerful look. Beds were for sleeping in so silence was expected of us. Not always so, of course. Rules were relaxed later on, when we were permitted to take a book to bed in the Summer. Bedtime was in relays according to age: 6 o'clock, 7 o'clock, 7.30 and so on. Strip wash, not forgetting the teeth and a bath once a week, sharing the water. Prayers before getting into bed. We rose early, about 6.45 a.m. Those of us who were old enough had a task before breakfast, sweeping, dusting or polishing—and done properly! Boots or shoes were polished outside in the playground and how cold it was in the Winter. We used a black block of something in a saucer to which was added a little water. Really quite hard work; then breakfast and change for school.

Our schoolroom was a lovely room away from the main building and reached by a covered way. It was kept warm in the Winter by an anthracite stove at each end of the room. It had a stage which we used frequently. Two classes sat each end of the room seated at long desks. Our teacher was a delightful person, and made lessons so interesting. She always looked so attractive, too. Thimble Pie was meted out occasionally if we forgot ourselves: a tap on the head with a thimble! In 1924, the committee decided that our lives would be broadened if we went outside to school and mixed with other children. We were received very kindly by teachers and children. I found myself back at the school I had left almost three years before and was quite embarrassed meeting old friends again. I recall a neighbour on his way to the Grammar School, used to greet me happily as I passed in crocodile to school. I didn't appreciate it one bit.

Our underwear composed of flannel vest, calico combinations, dark blue knickers with tape at waist and elastic at leg, all home-made. I learned herringbone stitch on the flannel vests! We wore black, home-knitted socks or stockings, there again we were taught to knit. In the earlier days, navy blue serge frocks with a strip of lace at neck and, of course, pinafores. Clothing was changed once a week, also handkerchiefs, but I found a means of washing and drying mine during the week. Outdoor clothes consisted of dark coloured coats and felt hats in all shapes and sizes. Not uniform. A different set for Sundays.

Straw hats in Summer, again, mixed and worn with dark dresses. Woollen gloves in Winter and cotton in Summer. We wore boots for a short while in my time, but later black lace-up shoes. We were taught to repair our own clothes as much as was possible. When we went out to school we wore homemade gym frocks, not the usual style, and blouses. I did feel out of place because we *did* look different from those who were not orphans. We did not attend the cinema, but always went to the Pantomime. A member of our committee belonged to the Swansea Operatic Society and through him we were invited to their dress rehearsals at the Y.M.C.A. At home, we used the playground for our play with balls and ropes and a great deal of make believe, which could work well as we were a group playing together. If weather did not permit we played in the schoolroom. For a whole month in the year, usually May, we took over a house in Horton, Gower. That was very exciting. Our luggage, which included mattresses and bedding, was taken down on a lorry. We travelled by private bus. Some of us slept two, three or four in the beds of the house, and the rest on mattresses on the floor, which served as a lovely base for playing 'Five Stones.' Silence was forgotten and freedom was the operative word. Food was much more interesting and I recall enormous boxes of oranges, one of which we received each day after dinner. Sweets, too, came our way and on Saturdays we went with our pocket money either to the Post Office (a rather grumpy Post Mistress. Maybe she didn't like children) or to a little shop in Port Eynon. Choosing the right sweet was the biggest task in the world. We bathed, had picnics on the beach, took walks through beautiful country lanes and picked flowers, which we pressed. The hedges in those days were profuse with wild flowers. Oh! They were lovely! Matron came along prepared with a whistle should any traffic come along. It would be out of the question today. When I look back on those holidays, nostalgia sets in. They were very happy days. I recall, too, how much closer we came to Matron, for she joined with us in most events. The staff on the whole were good to us. I do not recall any cruelty or special unkindness. A small spank (deserved) from time to time and a pinafore over the head facing the wall. Severe punishment was the cane meted out by Matron only. I do not feel resentment for these things, nevertheless.

Saturdays we rose later and after breakfast part of the morning was spent on extra cleaning of our schoolroom, cloakroom and wash place. The afternoons varied between walking to Swansea Bay, playing hockey amongst ourselves, to Singleton Park, and sometimes in the Summer an afternoon in the lovely garden of a committee member. He lived in Sketty. Wet days were spent in the schoolroom, but I do not remember much provision for that. We did have books to read. The weekly bath and to bed.

Sunday, later rising and the collect of day to be learned before breakfast, after which we changed for Church. Those who were confirmed went to early Communion. Dinner and Sunday School taken by an outsider, a lovely person. After tea, hymn singing until bedtime.

From time to time we put on plays and other entertainment with Matron's and outsider's help, so that we became familiar with many songs and poems. Our pianist was a friend of the home; he taught us the songs and accompanied us on the night. Also, we had a weekly session with a P.E. Teacher, who taught us simple gymnastics. It was all very enjoyable. It is evident to me now that Matron was constantly working hard to improve our lot.

Christmas was another happy occasion. Matron sent out letters appealing for donations towards it. I know, because after Christmas some of us were chosen to reply with thanks. A large Christmas tree beautifully decorated stood in the schoolroom and from which Father Christmas presented each of us with a gift. Our Christmas Eve gift was usually a useful article—brush and comb, toilet bag, sewing box, a book, etc., and a toy for the young ones. Christmas dinner and pudding with threepenny bits and charms for the lucky finders. I remember, too, we each had a new shilling. There were extras such as oranges and sweets and fun and games in the schoolroom when the staff and Matron joined us. We had many kind friends on that occasion. Looking back now in my years of wisdom, I know, that for all our restrictions and lack of parental love, we were very fortunate. We gained more than we lost. Maybe we were too protected for we had a certain naivety when just out in the world. Those days did leave some effect on me for it was many years before I admitted to anyone that I had been brought up in an orphanage. Now I am not concerned and feel it might have been an advantage.

After passing through the Housegirl period (I regretted having to leave school), I joined the staff and trained to be the Childrens' Attendant. During that period I became closer to Matron and realized what an amazing person she was. For all her sternness her heart was in her work and she was determined to improve the status of the home and did, eventually. She possessed great foresight and among her many attributes she was a wonderful nurse. To be ill was no tragedy for she cared well for us. She could diagnose the complaint as well as any doctor. I look back with great admiration for her. That is not to say that others do not think differently. Talking with one of my contemporaries last year, she was very bitter, 'tho life has treated her well.

JOHN PRIOR OF SWANSEA AND PORTH, RHONDDA

Born August 4th, 1914
Son of Archibald Frederick Prior and his wife
Mary Prior née Andrewartha

Both my parents were born in Swansea, South Wales, but my grandparents were all born in Cornwall. The family originated in Cornwall on both sides: we didn't consider ourselves Welsh. My great-grandfather William Andrewartha was Superintendent of Hafod Copper Works and a local Wesleyan Preacher; born in Breage he brought his wife and children to Wales. His son, my grandfather, was William John Andrewartha, who became Works Manager at Hafod. He died in 1894 of diabetes; his wife, after his premature death at the age of thirty-nine, was forced to become a housekeeper for Thomas the Jewellers, and later for a doctor who was a notorious drunkard and was later committed to a lunatic asylum. She, poor thing, died aged fifty-eight in 1911 of premature senility, and her daughter, my mother, after a brief period of mourning married Archibald Prior on January 2nd, 1912, at the Bible Christians Chapel. Her brothers thought it improper for her to marry in the same year as her mother's death, and so they waited for 1912.

The Priors were an interesting family. My great-grandfather, Michael Loam Prior, built steam engines; there is a tradition that he was a friend of Isambard Kingdom Brunel, and worked with him on the first iron ship. He was given Brunel's drawing tools. At this time the Priors lived at Saltash, but Michael travelled all over the world, taking his son John (my grandfather) with him. Eventually John settled down in Swansea as a station engineer, and operated the steam engine he'd helped to build as a young man. Upon his marriage to Emily Berryman, whose father was burnt to death in a bush fire in Australia after deserting his wife, he had to settle down to living a more sedate life.

Michael Loam Prior died in a mine accident, after falling down a shaft. He had also put in engines on the Rand Gold Mines in Africa. His son, John, brought gold back from Africa and my father had a gold watch chain made from this. Grandfather was an atheist and vegetarian, but became a Methodist under the influence of his wife Emily. He had only one lung and died of pneumonia the day that his son-in-law was being buried from the same house: he died as the coffin was being taken out.

I was born the day war was declared. We had a house on Burrows Road, near Swansea Bay. We lived on the first floor above the garage where the cars of Mr. Ernest Leeder, estate agent and antique dealer, were kept. My father had charge of the garage and maintenance of the cars: he was an automobile engineer. He also drove for Mr Leeder. As a very little boy I used to sit on a window seat at the front of the house where there was a view of the public house next door. I used to watch the horses and wagons delivering the beer. I was so interested in them, and nobody could understand why I knew about them.

My older sister Florence, born in 1912, loved me very much. As soon as I could stand up and walk, she'd dress me up and play with me as her baby. Some time at the end of 1914, our father volunteered in the Army. He was placed in the Army Service Corps, where he rose to be a sergeant-major. His particular work was with armoured trucks, lorries and cars. He maintained and operated a mobile repair truck which was used in France to rescue and rehabilitate lorries, supply and otherwise repair. He often had to work under fire as they were never far from the German lines. He was gassed, and also had some shrapnel wounds. One of the stories he told us was being on the battlefield at Loos when the Scots met the first attack of gas and were impaled on the barbed wire with their kilts draped around their heads, and their bare legs turning blue in death. Dad also, at one time, had a narrow escape when his truck left one door of the barn where they'd been sheltered, as the Germans arrived at the back door of the barn.

The only child born without a midwife was my brother Grenfell. Mother was completely alone in the house with two children, my sister and myself. Dad arrived home on leave the morning after the baby was born in May 1916. Before my father's return from the War we had moved to a small cottage on Castle Street, immediately in front of Oystermouth Castle. There we stayed until 1919 when the War was over and Dad was back in civilian life. It was a white cottage, part of a row with a garden at the back and an old apple tree growing over the loo.

I remember soldiers coming home on leave, and also military funerals with horses and gun carriages carrying the coffin through the street to the cemetery. Our neighbour's husband was brought back and buried in this way not long after he'd been home on leave.

During the War we would queue outside the grocery store to get our ration of sugar, and whatever else was available. Our neighbour volunteered to dig up the garden for mother, and planted vegetables. I used to play hide-and-seek between the rows of potatoes, and bury my face in the sweet smelling mint we grew.

One of the things we did quite often, was to take the Mumbles train to Swansea, where my parents' family lived. We'd visit Uncle William Andrewartha, who was proprietor of Victoria Cafe on St. Helen's Road, and manager of Swansea Football Team. (He was also caterer to the Patti Pavilion.) The train we went on was the old type of steam engine called by us, Puffing Billy, pulling carriages that looked like tram cars, which made a regular route between Swansea town and the Mumbles. I always had a great deal of trouble because I was always sick riding in the top, and the smoke from the engine used to blow on us and we'd be covered with black cinders at the end of each trip.

These were the days when we used to go past Singleton Abbey, used, I believe, as a hospital for wounded soldiers. We used to see soldiers on crutches and in bandages, taking their exercise by walking on the promenade. The soldiers wore blue shirts and red ties as a hospital uniform. My mother made me a blue shirt and I wore a red tie with it. Another thing I remember, is going with mother and two other children down to one of the bays and seeing a German ship which had run aground: that's all I remember, but it was a sight I never have forgotten. Fishing boats still went out from the little ports with red sails, dark red they were. Old sailors with navy blue jerseys and peaked caps sat around on old boats in the sun and swapped stories.

I went to school when I was four years old. Then I began to learn how to do things. It seems to me that it must have been a school of the Montessori method: because we learned by doing.

In 1918, when peace came, we went to Birmingham for Christmas, staying with mother's aunt Mrs. James Davies. We called her Aunt Marie, although everyone else called her Aunt Polly. We were there when soldiers were coming back from overseas, some of them bringing German helmets and gas masks with them. It was after this visit that Dad came home and we moved to Porth. It was 1919 and I was four years old.

Porth is at the junction of the Rhondda Valley—the two rivers, the Rhondda Fach and the Rhondda Mawr, come together at Porth—which means 'gateway to the valley.' The river flows to Pontypridd where it joins the Taff, which flows to Cardiff. The children in Porth seemed, for the most part, to have a somewhat rougher life. They played very much easier than our cousins seemed to do. Also, of course, the clothing was a little different. Hobnails were plentiful in Porth. Didn't see many of those in Swansea.

Now I was sent to the Infants School. We began with letters and sounds, only this time in Welsh as well as English. The mistress came outside and rang a big brass bell when it was time to go in. The playground was covered with gravel. Our school was separated from the Elementary School by a high stone wall. The name of the school was Llwyncellyn. We learned reading, arithmetic and singing in Welsh and English, and art (drawing). Everyday there was a scripture lesson with the stories from the Old and New Testament, not read, but told by the teachers. Two little Jewish children always sat outside the door during the lessons. I don't remember anyone praying.

The things I enjoyed most were reading and the art. We used the art in very simple geography lessons, drawing the shapes of countries, and also the things we imagined to be in those countries, such as animals. I advanced my reading with two or three other members of the class, so that we finished our reading books and were, from then on, excused from reading classes and allowed to meet with the headmistress. We sat with her, and were given advanced books to read; allowed to read on our own, once a week, not reporting, but telling her what we'd read for content. We also had the opportunity to read aloud.

The arithmetic lesson was the regular add and subtract apples and pears. Discipline was very strict in the sense that children were to remain quiet, and if for any reason teachers left the room, a monitor was appointed to take the names of those who talked or moved. There was a thing about being late. You were punished by having to stand outside the headmistress's door. Every teacher had a thin bamboo cane which hung on a nail in the classroom, and was used by slapping across the palm of the hand. I remember once being caned for lateness. The punishment teacher was a man, and he gave me—no excuses accepted—four cracks with that cane and raised blisters on my hand. My father, immediately I showed him, went to school and I was never caned again.

We were never really aware of very much truancy but, of course, knew that it sometimes happened, but most children in our school area seemed to have good attendance records. I can't remember anyone I knew who consistently missed school. Many were tardy and paid the penalty of one crack across the palm of the hand with the bamboo cane: if often late, the punishment was increased. There was a certain Mr. Harris that everyone hated—he was a brutal man.

St. David's Day was celebrated in great detail. We all wore daffodils; some of those whose parents grew them, leeks. Boys loved chewing on the green leaves all through school. There was a gathering in the large hall of our school and a programme of singing and reciting in Welsh. All of us were in groups and sang in competition, as in the Eisteddfod. We also submitted drawings of daffodils, etc. The girls all made small bags and they also were adjudicated. Prizes were given; a threepenny bit, perhaps, or the grand sixpence, and each prize winner had the award in a bag. We had a splendid time. I sang with a group and also won prizes for my drawing. School was dismissed for a half holiday— we thoroughly enjoyed the day.

We were allowed to play outside in the street; our terrace street was a dead-end and little traffic moved. Horses carted coal from the tipple up our street. In order for the carts to get up hills, extra horses were used in the harnesses with chains for pulling. We knew the carters and usually were able to have rides on horses being taken to use in this manner. In front of our house was a grassy bank, belonging to the colliery. We also had a cricket field, used also for football, and the ever present tip where the mine waste was piled. We used all these resources in our free time. Mother and Dad were quite willing for us to play with the neighbours' children and we spent wonderful days together, friends, hiking over the mountains and carrying our haversacks, drinking water out of clear cold springs and eating cheese sandwiches. We also built dugouts, lit fires, baked potatoes and sang and jumped and played.

The Elementary School (on the other side of the wall to the infants) we approached through another gate. There, each morning when the bell rang, we lined up by classes, and marched into the cloakroom: a dismal room with stands to hang your coats and caps, and washbasins which never worked. It was there that we inherited head lice from all the miners' children whose caps were next to ours. Mother combed our hair with a fine-tooth comb every night. We leaned over a big china bowl: if we had any head lice they fell in the bowl and were exterminated. Mother always called them 'elephants'.

In the Elementary School, our teacher was a Mr. William Lewis, a middle-aged bachelor. A man whose training was purely in the local normal school (no degree), stayed with the class as we came along through the next three or four years. He was a wonderful man and had a great understanding of young children. He dramatized the history lessons, told us little anecdotes and side stories. He also allowed us to dramatize the poems and parts of Shakespeare that we had in our reading class. This man gave us all a vision, and opened up doors for our imagination. He talked to us as individuals. Those of us who were able to advance faster than others were given advanced work to do. While the slow ones laboured, we went on further than our books allowed. He gave us special problems.

Perhaps, as the only English boy (even though I was second generation Welsh, I was still regarded as a 'stranger'), he did not push me on Welsh. Although I had a smattering of the meaning of words, he did not expect me to converse in Welsh. We all had to recite Welsh poetry and sing Welsh songs. Every day there was dictation. We wrote down what he read out, with proper spellings and punctuation. Each Friday morning we had tests in Arithmetic, English and Dictation, and were seated in the order of our marks. There were about thirty to thirty-five in our class, half and half, girls and boys. The girls never seemed to be as advanced as the boys.

On Friday afternoons we all listened to records on the school gramaphone. It was a time of general relaxation before we went home. Classes began at 8.45 a.m. and ceased at noon, home for lunch, then we returned for 1.30 p.m. and stayed in school until 4 p.m. Most people had dinner at noon.

One of the things that always puzzled me as a child, in 1921, was that nearly everyone, except for a very few of us, brought bowls and spoons to school every day. This was also true in 1926. The answer, of course, was that they went to the Soup Kitchen for their dinner because of the General Strike. At what was dinner time—noon—they went down to the Tin Chapel and had soup from the helpers down there. This Tin Chapel was a nonconformist chapel of some kind of Welsh Baptists.

We *were* conscious of political differences. Our parents were Conservative. We were able to read the Western Mail at an early age, so there were things of which we were aware. Up our stret, some twenty or so houses along, the General Secretary of the Miners' Union had his home; he was, as a matter of fact, a cousin of our next door neighbour Mrs. Rhys Jones, and his name was A.J. Cook. I remember seeing him from time to time walking down the road. He was very popular with many of the people, but feelings were also strong in those who did not agree with the way the Labour Party was going. There was a lot of talk about *Bolshies* and newspaper cartoons always showed them carrying *bombs*. I can remember talk by children in school that Mr. Cook had been to Russia to get his *instructions*. These were difficult times and families were split. The managers were not at all happy with the strikers, and yet I cannot remember any confrontations or physical encounters.

I do remember when, in the progress of the 1926 strike, one of the under managers, another Mr. Jones, was killed by a rock fall underground. His body was carried on a stretcher down our street from the mine, and I heard someone say:

"It serves him right for not going on strike".

Now this was the father of one of our friends and we all felt very badly. Also, the miners wanted all of the people, like my father who was a manager, to help support the Soup Kitchens by giving part of their weekly wages to help. They made the mistake in the colliery offices of subtracting a certain percent from the wages of each working official. My father hit the roof and bitterly took action. He said that he also had a family and if he wanted to help, he would, but no one was going to take his money without his permission. I think he won the battle. At least, we never heard about it again. Most of the miners lived in row houses belonging to the Colliery and kept up by a staff that continued in repairs and upkeep. I can't remember anyone being evicted from non-payment of rent.

One of the problems was fuel. Coal was the usual heating and cooking agent. The Colliery supplied coal to people at a low rate, but not during the strike, unless of dire emergency. The men of our area went out on the tips that surrounded the Colliery and dug up the coal that was present in the waste. The whole place became like a bombed area with large pits and holes. No-one from the management stopped them and, while it meant heavy work, most people managed to stay warm and were able to cook meals.

I remember the 1926 strike very well. At first, all the Unions in the country went on strike. The first day, the Government took over and within a few days things were working all over the country. Then the other Unions went back to work and the coal miners stayed on strike; some men were never able to work again for the rest of their lives. Coal lost its importance as oil became the fuel of the ships and many other industries were founded on the use of oil. In all, we came through these days with no ill feeling between ourselves and our Welsh neighbours; we respected each other and loved those who lived as we did. I know that there must have been a great deal of ill will on both sides. However, we Cornish people endured and, whilst living among the coal mines was not the most pleasant time, we had, and have, no regrets.

Yes, we children had our jobs to do at home. I don't know when it started. Grenfell and I cleaned the silver on Saturday with whiting. Then the dinner knives which were not stainless steel were rubbed with some kind of brick. We hosed down the courtyard at the back of the house and cleaned out the dog kennel: we had two Welsh terriers. I can't remember what the girls did. On Fridays father gave us a penny each, so on Saturday afternoon we went to the matinee at the cinema.

132

Going to the movies was quite important in our family. Mother and Dad enjoyed going out together and, of course, when they wanted to do so there was little other entertainment in Porth. When they went up to London, and for some years this was an annual event, the Motor Show was important and they went to the Music Halls and other productions, but in Porth, they went to the cinema. Dad always bought mother some chocolates and off they went like a couple of our modern teenagers. There were at least three cinemas open and I remember when a new one was opened in the late Twenties; somewhere around 1926. The cheapest and most primitive place was called, in polite terms, the 'Pictorium.' It was run by a friend of mine's parents. The seats were long benches without backs, and the place was made dark at the time of the movie by closing large shuttered windows. Order was kept very strictly and the movies, of course, were the old silents. It was there we saw Charles Chaplin and all the others in the early Twenties, as we went to matinees on Saturday afternoon. Dad always provided the pennies for entrance; it cost just that, a penny. It was also called the 'Rink.' At one time it had been a skating rink, but that would have been before our time. The neighbouring young people saw that we children, Florence, Grenfell and I, were well taken care of.

In the very centre of town there were two more theatres; one called the Central and the other the Grand. The Grand was usually referred to as 'Bug Palace.' It was very popular and shows were quite up to the times. It was in the middle of a row of shops and backed onto a bakery; there was usually a lovely odour of fresh bread and we all rather enjoyed that.

After a while, Dad decided that we should be going to the Central, a better and higher form of theatre. It cost 2d. and we usually sat upstairs in the first row of the balcony. The show fare was as much up-to-date as possible and we were quite interested in the more sophisticated products of Hollywood; Adolphe Menjou was a familiar person. It was quite nice to go into a comfortable, good smelling building, without the crowds of noisy street urchins. Also, the manager had a daughter in my class in school and I was quite attracted by her. Alas, after a while they moved back to London and, of course, we came to America.

I suppose the Westerns were the most interesting films and, of course, the Serials; each week we waited for the heroine to be saved from death, or a fate worse than death, whatever that was in our young lives. Grenfell never walked anywhere and always galloped. He sat in the seat warning the enemies and rapidly drawing his pistols, (utterly imaginative) to defend the innocent and proud young heroes. He was quite vocal and embarrassed us a little as he spent his time shooting the 'Ku Klux Klan' or as he always called them, 'The Holy Terrors.' How these afternoons had any kind of influence on us, I just can't say. However, they did work on our imagination, and we furthered the somewhat doubtful American entertainment by doing a great deal of reading. We all read from the day we were able, and we read everything readable that came into our hands. It might be strange, too, in a way, that our branch of the family were able to attend movies, while some of our relatives were still not sure that it was a Christian thing to do. We were very fortunate indeed in our parents. They were not tied down by much of what passed for Welsh Methodist piety—we were, indeed, free. Some of our cousins were tied down to an old type Methodism.

In our house we always had help. We had a girl come in to do the general cleaning every day and help take care of the children. Mother did most of the cooking. Another woman came in and did the laundry. Housekeeping meant black leading grates, scrubbing floors on hands and knees: our floors were red tile on the ground floor, excepting in the kitchen where they were quarried paving stones. The tiled floors were blood-red and were waxed with Mansion polish with throw-rugs over them. The brass was polished: there was a lot of brass in the house.

In Porth, we had a seven room house with a bathroom, the only one in our row. That was because of Dad's job as manager. The Colliery owned the house and we had one extra room because of Dad's position. In the kitchen there were double ovens, one on each side of the grate. We also had double ovens in the dining-room. There was hot water heated by the fireplace by a damper which burned coal from the Colliery at special prices.

Each fireplace in our house was complete with fender and fireguard, fire-dogs and fire tools. We had fires in the kitchen, dining-room and sitting-room, when using it. We discovered that the miners' wives made a type of coal bag up. Our neighbours collected the tea leaves from the tea pot over a period of time, then mixed it with the small coal and put the mixture back into the teabag the grocer had given them: this was then used with the proper coal to keep the fire going. We never did this. The only time we had fires upstairs was when someone was ill. We had three bedrooms. The bathroom had been put in especially for us when we came. It was large, with an alcove sometimes used as a bedroom; there was a double bed with a curtain.

Our laundress came in on a Monday and spent the day. Our favourite was Lizzy Harris. We had big boilers which were carried out into the yard. There was a stone slab with a tub, and the clothes were mangled: we had a new mangle with rubber rollers. Lizzy the laundress was a great talker, we loved to listen to her telling stories about her family and school; she'd be about fifteen or sixteen. Mother trained girls from the family next door, who came to our house and learned how to keep house. Each of the girls in turn went into domestic service in larger houses as cook, general servant and housekeeper. One was a cook at Eton. We loved them. When we went to the pantomime, father always saw we took them with us. We lived among the miners and they were our friends, even though we were separated from them by a different kind of life.

There was no electricity in our house, just gas-lights with a meter in the alcove in the parlour, with a bowl of pennies that came in handy. Grenfell used to nick a penny every now and then to buy Woodbine cigarettes, which I helped him to smoke away from the house.

My father was not home very much. He had taken on a job as manager of the garage at the Colliery, and after the War many things had been neglected. Bringing things up-to-date, and doing repairs kept him busy most nights. Then, on most weekends, he was required to drive the general manager of the Colliery, Mr. Percy Osborne Ward. He had been a colonel in the Indian Army and had his home in Merthyr. He and father were friends. They went away together on weekends on fishing trips: father would drive out of town in his chauffeur's uniform, then change. They'd go fishing or shooting together and stay in houses. We had rabbits, trout and salmon hanging in our pantry.

Our parents were affectionate, like sweethearts. My father always bought chocolates for mother, and always brought her something when he'd been away. They went to the theatre like a couple of youngsters. We always knew they loved each other. Each year, Dad went to the Motor Show with Mr. Ward. Mother went, too, as a guest. They'd leave him in London and come home together in the Rolls, staying at inns and going to the theatre. The girls next door stayed with us. I think my father worshipped my mother: they'd known each other since childhood.

We used to have an early bedtime and as we got older, father was home more often, especially after Mr. Ward died. Our parents went to whist drives and to friends' houses for dinners. They also entertained. One New Year's Eve they went to Church, to the Midnight Watchnight Service, and the curate and several other couples came home with them for a late roast duck dinner. Also, my father and mother taught the oldest of us to play whist, and so we spent evenings playing together.

Our parents became interested in the Anglican Church whilst we lived in Porth, but were not confirmed until we were in America. We always had blessings and prayers before bedtime.

As a family we spent a lot of time together; holidays, picnics on the mountains. They played with us and read with us, mostly mother as father was often away. But Dad taught me to play dominoes, draughts and cribbage. He also bought us target pistols and rifles. He took us to museums. He was a good father, but didn't know how to deal with boys.

Christmas was a great thing in our family. The children and maid festooned the kitchen with ivy. We made paper ornaments and lanterns. My father brought home all sorts of Christmas goodies: the sideboard was filled with fruit, nuts, chocolates, nougats, nonpareils, and jubes. We didn't have turkey, we had goose: father carved and the table was set in the dining-room with linen tablecloth and napkins.

Mother worked for weeks making puddings and cakes for Christmas. When we were old enough we all shared in stoning raisins and blanching nuts and then the final stir of the pudding before placing it into basins. The cakes were taken to the local bakery to be baked. I'll never forget getting our cakes with the maid: there was a delicious smell. Mother always made one round cake which father iced with almond and royal icing, and decorated with cashews and leaves of different coloured icing. There were always mince pies, lemon curds and blackberry jam tarts. We did not have Christmas trees. In our neighbourhood I only know one person who did, and all the children in the neighbourhood asked to see it; a small live one in a tub decorated with real candles.

On Christmas Eve we hung our stocking up, and the next morning at each table place at breakfast, you would find your gift. Our stockings usually contained: an orange, apple, nuts, hankies, small toys and candy-canes (rock). I always remember one of our neighbours whose father had brought home chocolate cordials which contained real liqueur: he nicked them out of his mother's room and entertained us at school with a taste of them, until he got caught. We always had people come to visit, family from Swansea. All this was done on Dad's salary which was about three pounds a week.

In the winter we had porridge for breakfast, then other times toast, bread and jam. On special occasions a boiled egg and only very occasionally, bacon. For lunch, well it depended on the day: on Saturday, pasties; Sunday a roast with dried peas and rice pudding; Monday always cold meat, boiled potatoes, vegetables and apple tart; Tuesday, hash; Wednesday, liver, tripe and onions, sometimes a stew, sausages very rarely; Friday, usually fish. For tea there would be cold meats, bread and butter, tarts, cakes, stewed fruits, custards, trifles, jellies, blancmanges and junkets with clotted cream on top. When father was in Cornwall he would send home pints of clotted cream by post. We never ate chops, mince or steaks. We did have rabbits and boiled ham. Steak and kidney pie was considered a special treat.

Each day there was a regular procession of people selling things in carts on the street; vegetables and fish. A milk-maid would come each morning wearing a yoke across her shoulders with a milk can at each end and the milk would be dipped out for us.

There was fresh fruit all the time: great supplies of apples and pears. Eggs were not plentiful. We were always given a slice of bread and jam before going to bed. Our parents would have their supper about ten o'clock. They had cold meat, pickles and cheese. Mother always had tea in bed in the morning before breakfast. As we boys grew older we came down, made the tea, buttered crackers and took it up to them.

Our family was a close-knit unit, but the neighbours were important because when father was away a man was needed for the heavy jobs. Mr. Rhys Jones, our neighbour, whose daughters worked for us, always came over and split the kindling for the fire and carried down the coal. He also dug the garden. My father used to give him books and magazines as he was a great reader. Mrs. Jones kept her eye open and made sure mother was comfortable. She helped in many ways, but never stayed in the house when father was around.

Most holidays we went to Swansea, spending a week or so there. We went by train: most of the time my father wasn't with us. Much of the time was spent visiting relatives and also visiting beaches around Gower. We were all great walkers. Each summer there was a great exodus of people from Porth, all the Sunday Schools went on day excursions to places like Barry Island. There were day trips as a family to Penarth, charabanc to Porthcawl. I was so young at the time, I didn't realise why we stopped so many times and all the men got out.

At the time our hobbies were hiking and boy scouts. We collected cigarette cards, which were used as an exchange among us boys and there was various kinds of gambling. We were also vitally interested in fossils, and living in Porth, the centre of the coal mining area, we had ample opportunity to find splendid specimens from the tips where the mine tailings were piled. We had a very unusual collection of beautiful ferns and plants.

During the Strike of 1926, the miners spent most of their time preparing and taking part in band competitions. Each small community, or section, had their own band. They dressed in costumes and played, for the most part, kazoos disguised as musical instruments. These contests were held all over the valley; they called themselves Jazz Bands, competing, of course. There were all kinds of male bands: the Britannia Golliwogs, all dressed up like golliwogs; Llyncellan Pierrots, and the Tonypandy Turkish Band, dressed up like harem girls, provided music with nose whistlers and whatever anyone else could think of— westerners, easterners, orientals. Some remarkably clever ones had special drill teams to do movements. All our communities were entertained. The strikers enjoyed it all, too, it gave them a certain freedom that they did not know down the mines. People had a good laugh. I don't think that the area we lived in was as deeply touched by the Red Issue as many have believed.

My father was regarded by the neighbours as a superior being. We had very little to do with the people around us. Dad dressed differently; no cap or muffler, always properly attired with a trilby or bowler. They were in awe of him as a manager and official of the mine. This was a society of underlings. The social life of the miners really was a mystery to us. We used to be amazed to see little children standing outside pubs on a Saturday night, waiting for their parents to come out.

We never wore hand-me-downs. Mother would never allow us to have hobnail boots like the rest of the miners' sons. We wore boots without hobnails, and Oxford shoes on Sunday. We boys were horrified one time when Mother outfitted us in especially nice outfits with straw hats and patent leather strapped shoes—sailor suits. Mother always removed the whistle. I often wore Eton collars and bow ties with a short jacket and combinations known as 'bum-freezers.' We had Norfolk jackets and tan raincoats with caps to match. Always short pants.

In 1922 or '23 we had the first wireless in our area. It was made by a friend of father's. We had a big aerial in the garden, powered by batteries that had to be constantly re-charged: in the beginning it only had earphones. Later on, we had a speaker shaped like a horn, almost like a gramophone. We used to listen every evening: people stood outside to listen.

In 1925, the general manager, Percy Osborne Ward, died suddenly. My father, who had tied his future to Mr. Ward's, was at a loss. He and Mr. Ward had always planned that when Mr. Ward retired in a year or two, that father would manage his estate, and the country house had already been bought in Abergavenny, and a house provided for all of us to move into. But this all came to an end, for although Mr. Ward had amply provided for my father in his will (an estate valued at £100,000), he died before he was able to sign it. By this time, things in Wales were economically poor. There seemed to be no future, and although his job

139

was secure, the old friendship had gone. There was no real future for us as a family in that area.

The decision to go to America was not an easy one because my father really wanted to stay in the British Empire. He wrote to people in Canada, Australia, New Zealand and South Africa. The reason we didn't go to one of these British Colonies was, although they were sending immigrants out, what they really needed, and were prepared to assist, were farmers—my father was not a farmer!

We had contact with America through my father's aunt who had married a Mr. Richards and who had moved to Youngstown, Ohio in the 1880s. At the time, Mr. Richards was still alive, although he was an elderly man. His son, Simon, corresponded with father. We were encouraged by the word that employment could be found and also, in those days, one could not emigrate to America except under the quota system which America allowed, and had to be able to provide a statement that one would not become a public charge. The simple fact was, that while one could not go to a job, your relative could sponsor you and supply a statement that they would support you if you were unable to support yourself. After all these papers were signed, your name was put on the immigration list.

It took eighteen months before our name came up. During that time I had passed my eleven plus and had scholarships in both the Secondary and Intermediate schools, which were both turned down because we thought we'd be going to America. The result was, I took the exams and received two new scholarships and began the Intermediate school in September 1927. Almost immediately we were notified that our number had come up and we motored to Southampton to the American Consulate, in the general manager's car, for our medical examinations. We were somewhat embarrassed when they examined our hair for lice. After all the forms had been properly filled in, my father was asked if he could read and write. Also each child was independently asked the same question. We passed the examination on the 10th November, 1927 and that night, before we returned home, father contacted the Cunard Line in Southampton and secured passage on the S.S. Ascania for the 25th of November. At the time when Father was thinking of going to America, he said to Mother, "I'll go over and make a place for you and then send for you." My Mother said, "Archie, if I don't go with you, I'm not coming".

We returned home, took part in the Armistice Day Service; Florence, Grenfell and I sang in the choir; we notified the school authorities of our plans and began to dispose of our furniture. Father had a chest built by the carpenters of the colliery with rope handles, and on the 25th the general manager's chauffeur drove us to Cardiff in the Sunbeam and we took the train to Southampton, arriving in the evening.

We had been in Swansea in 1926 for Christmas with Mother's brothers and so did not return again. Mother's china—antique Wedgewood and Crown Derby—was bought by the general manager's wife, so that paid for our passage. It was a 'farewell Wales' and 'Hail America.' A completely new way of life was about to start which bore no relationship to the one we had in Porth. At twelve years of age I landed in the States: it was not like the films.[1]

---

[1] The Priors sailed on the S.S. Ascania, launched in 1925 and so still very new. John was eventually to become the Very Reverend John Prior, Dean of Florence and Rector of St. Bartholomew's Church, Hartsville, South Carolina.

VIOLET LORRAINE NORMAN OF LLANELLI

Born January 21st, 1917
The daughter of James Henry Norman and his wife
Isabella Norman, née Davies.

My parents had left Cardigan to find work. My grandfather had preceded them and they followed him to Llanelli as it was a boom town: a tinplate town. It was the Mecca for employment. People left the land to get jobs in the docks: there were three of them—North, South and Nevill's (which also had a foundry). It was in the docks that my father found employment. Men came to work in the steelworks, brickworks, tinworks and in the chemical industry. A network of G.W.R. lines ran through them all. Even the main street in Llanelli, Station Road, had large works on either side: trucks and wagons criss-crossed the road.

Although my mother was a *Cardi*, born in Cardiganshire, the daughter of a Welsh sea captain on the river Teify, my father was a Bristolian, and they married at Verwig, Cardigan. Mam was brought up a Baptist. As a young woman she went to the hiring fair in Cardigan to be hired out to a farmer. She worked at several farms. At one place, the main and only meal consisted of potatoes mashed with buttermilk: that was all she got. The work was hard and lasted from early light until dusk. When my mother married they went to live in the centre cottage of three at the Netpool in Cardigan. I was the first child to be born in Llanelli. The town was an entirely new world for my parents and my brothers and sisters who were Cardigan born: it was a world of noise and activity.

Our house was on Biddulph Street, New Dock, number eleven, and consisted of a parlour, a living room and back kitchen. Attached to the back kitchen was a large outhouse with a fireplace used for keeping the wooden tub in, with washing board and dolly. We used the dolly to pound the washing with, then out on to the washing board with its brass corrugated surface. This *twba* was also used on bath nights: it was brought into the kitchen and put in front of the fire. But our father bought a newfangled large oval tin bath which could hold three girls at the same time. This saved waiting for the kettle to boil all the time. There were three bedrooms in the house: one for our parents, one for the two boys, and the largest one had two beds in it for the girls. Night time was fun time with pillow fights and bed bouncing: until father's step could be heard on the stairs. Then we all pretended to be asleep. Looking back I wonder how my mother could put up with us all. The landlord of our rented house was a Theophilus Jenkins. Around our area were Welsh, English, Irish, Scots, Jews and roaming gypsies. There was a daily ritual on the street: the house mats had to be shaken first thing in the morning. Then the step and pavement outside had to be scrubbed clean before noon (and heaven help anyone who walked over while you were scrubbing the flags. A wet floor cloth would probably catch them around the earhole).

Our house was terraced. There were several streets, all back-to-back with a back lane dividing them. The streets were gaslighted. In the evening the lighter-upper came with a long pole to turn up the gas. In the morning he set them out. Around the lamplight was a play area, it was outside the chip shop that had pride of place in the centre of our street. Sometimes a man would show up dressed like Charlie Chaplin: he would stand under the lamppost and entertain us. The hurdy-gurdy organ would come around. And the baker's handcart. Friday night was faggots and pease night.

Our father did have an allotment, and we had a large garden with chickens at one end of it. He also cobbled our boots on a last and soled and heeled them. He also shopped at the market late on Friday and Saturday nights for buys that were cheap and plentiful. We were like other families in bad times and sat down to a rabbit dinner: rabbits being the cheapest buy, lamb was second. Of course, there was always *cawl*, the Welsh soup: that was on the menu often with different variations according to what was available. My mother added a herb called *Safri Fach* (savory): it's a lovely herb. There were suet puddings, suety duff, and potato pie. There were trollies—suet pudding made in large shallow baking tins and served with treacle or golden syrup.

Coal was burnt in the grate if you could afford it. The clinker tips saw hordes of children with a sack, scraper and a bucket, all scraping for clinker *cols* which would burn. These tips were meant to be out of bounds and one was fined if caught collecting *cols*. No-one was allowed on the tips. Though living down by the sea, as a child, I never really saw the bay until some years ago when the two very high clinker barricades (which served as wind and sea breakers) were bulldozed down. In the home, fires had to be kept burning all the time. Heavy cast iron kettles full of water meant that boiling water was to be had almost all day.

Children were expected to help in the house. Women were very houseproud. Tables had to be scrubbed clean; linen kept white; brass all shining; black fireplaces polished with *Zebra*. Some girls worked very hard. My friend Ginny had lots of brothers and often had a whole *twba* full of clothes to wash: often she could not come out to play. All of Monday was wash day: from morn 'til night. Scrub wash in the *twba* then wring through the mangle, then dry out in the garden in a long row on the clothes line. No woman worked outside the home unless she was of single status. Marriage was full time. Some families were twelve or more children. My Mam had eleven, all boisterous. If she fell ill the older children took over so our Dad did not lose any work: we could not afford it. Mam's character was strong, but her body not so, not after all that childbearing. She used to tell us many stories of her young days: the trouble is we never listened to half. She sang all the hymns to us. One of her favourite songs, which I never hear today was '*Unwaith eto Cymru Annwyl*'.

When my mother's mother died, soon after childbirth, my mother being the youngest, was taken into the home of her aunt, Mrs. Venables. Now Mr. Venables liked his drink. It spoiled family life. And so my mother made certain that when she married it would be to a non-drinker. My father was teetotal.

After Church on Sundays, the vicar, a hunch-back called Mr. Jones, would visit every house in the street immaterial of denomination, and spend a few minutes chatting with the family. If one of the girls happened to be doing some urgent sewing on the machine it would be hastily hidden away out of sight as soon as it was known that the vicar was coming. Any kind of work on Sunday was sinful. We all attended the church opposite our house, Church of England, although I also went with my friends to the Baptists, Methodists and Independents. The only place I never got round to was the Synagogue: though I had lots of school friends who were Jewish. This was probably because Saturday was their religious day and I had too many other activities.

We had school and after school games. We had a lively ball game where the ball is bounced against a wall, lightly, with a count of ten, if dropped, 'out.' After a count of ten, nine, overhead, back to the wall a foot from it; if successful, eight under right arm, seven under left arm; six behind the back—difficult that one; five under left leg, four under right leg; three bouncing from rear between straddled legs; two, eyes shut; one, circle yourself with the bouncing ball without moving; then throw against the wall. Complete all those without dropping the ball and you were the winner. There were quoits, put-and-take (numbered and spun). Girls in a circle, one in the centre: she drops a handkerchief and someone in the circle picks it up and conceals it. The girl in the centre pretends to look for it: then circles the girls pointing at each one and singing

> I sent a letter to my love
> And on the way I lost it.
> One of you, must have picked it up
> And put it in your pocket.
> (Pointing at each girl in turn)
> It was you.

When she found the girl who had the handkerchief they would exchange places.

May Day at school was a big celebration. We wore white dresses, white socks and white plimsolls and danced around a Maypole. Sometimes there would be Morris Dancing. School was compulsory at five, but they would accept pupils from three years old. In the first classes we all chanted the alphabet. We sang a song, an action song: hands on the head, then on the shoulders; twiddle the fingers, then twiddle the thumbs. There were other action songs. Our nursery rhymes were all acted out and sung. Dancing was expression and exercise with the teacher calling out, "Point your toes now, girls".

We had slates and pencils, or slates and chalk to write on. There was drawing, clay work, mat making, raffia work, knitting and crochet.

After infants, it was primary school where learning began in earnest. Pupils had to be taught, like it or not. School inspectors came around, always unexpectedly, and observed a class at work without being seen by the teacher or the pupils, until he was prepared to make his presence known to them. I went to New Dock Infants, New Dock Girls, Coleshill and Prospect Place. Discipline was maintained mostly by loss of privileges, or being given lines, or detention, or black marks. The cane was used. There *were* parents who thought education unnecessary and a waste of time: looking at it from the point of view that all one needed was a good pair of hands and a steady eye. Education was compulsory and the whipper-in saw to it that children attended school. Parents could be fined or jailed if a child did not go. We sisters walked a mile and a half to the top school, then back home for dinner, so it was four times a day: six miles. It was an extra walk when we went to Prospect Place once a week for additional lessons like needlework, artwork, gymnastics and housewifery. The housewifery classes consisted of cooking, and also washing small items: tea towels, hand towels, handkerchiefs, and if you didn't bring your own dirty washing the teacher provided some.

Schools had so many rules. No-one liked going. There were nature walks through Stradey Woods, where the teacher might often lose half her pupils and the rest were sent to go hunting for them. A Miss Pickering came once to give us a lecture on Alcoholism: afterwards we had to put into our own words what we had heard and listened to. Hard luck on those who hadn't listened and could not write the essay.

Teachers being attacked by parents were not often recorded in girls sections, but we heard of boys being whipped a bit too hard and parents going up the school. The attitude of parents at that time was, "He wouldn't be here if it were not compulsory".

Children played truant because they would much rather be out in the fields assisting in bringing in the hay or helping on the farm which they thought more interesting. Or they played truant if they were bored and thought it all a waste of time. Punishments could be sadistic.

St. David's Day was celebrated by singing and then a dancing display. Empire Day would be celebrated, too, with schools all marching and banners waving with the band playing. Once we spent months preparing for a school concert to be performed before the whole school, plus parents. Later on we went to the Old Peoples' Hospital at Bryntirion to put our show on there: we performed on planks put across trestles. It made a rather shaky platform that bounced up and down by the energetic efforts of the performers.

The dentist came to the school and took teeth out there, at school, and so we dreaded his visits. School doctors examined the children and marked their weight and height on a card. It was a time of meningitis, scarlet fever, whooping cough and tuberculosis. Not far from our home was the Isolation Hospital for cases with contagious diseases to be sent to. We were thin, timid children. I doubt if there were fat pupils, except someone who was fat because of a health problem.

School inspections took place every morning of our lives. We lined up, showed our hands face-up, then nail inspection, and handkerchief inspection. Hair inspection was left to the Nurse who came around without warning every so often. Boys had neck and behind the ears inspection. The school had a cold, chill atmosphere. In the winter there were coal-fired stoves, but only to be lit when it was really cold, not before. Morning assemblies were lectures on inner cleanliness and the importance of Godliness.

My older sisters bought and exchanged romantic novels. I read them on the sly. *Peg's Paper*. My parents did not approve of trash novels, therefore all the girls read them in out of the way places such as the Bulwark Embankment, or the garden shed, or the lav at the bottom of the garden. Our lav was a wooden seat over a bucket container which was emptied into a hole at the bottom of the garden, then treated with lime. The lav was a private retreat. Often, I went down there with a novel: it was somewhere safe to read, write, or have a sly smoke for some girls who were daring enough to try it. When I was a girl, older ones were Flappers,[1] trying to capture the style of the moment, and sporting a long bone cigarette holder with all the mannerisms of being the elegant whiffer. Cigarettes were not encouraged by my father.

---

[1] Flapper is an interesting word. In the 1770s it was used to describe a young wild duck. By the 1900s it was used to describe a young girl who had not yet 'put her hair up' and also suggested flightiness. After the Great War it usually meant a young woman who had cut her hair short, who flouted decorum and tended to be more free and easy in her behaviour.

Our father was a volunteer Fireman. He had been involved in so much fire fighting, and seen so many tragedies, that he knew how easily fires can start. Woe betide us if we were caught with fags or matches. He himself, smoked a careful pipe: knocking out the ash very carefully into the fire. Once, one of the children bought a box of coloured matches, and was carelessly striking and holding them whilst they flared and hissed. Dad was very angry and threatened the strap if matches were ever bought again. He could never impress upon us enough the dangers of fire and the kind of burns one could suffer from it. Once, he was called out to a fire in Felinfoel where five children were burnt to death in horrific circumstances.

We girls tried to make a lot of things. The market sold lots of cheap materials. Girls made their own dresses, hats, bags and knitted things to wear. Annie, one of my sisters, could make excellent string bags and hair snoods. She could also make rush and raffia baskets and crochet dresses, vests and slips.

Christmas time arrived after months of excitement of looking ahead. Shops were filled with toys, books and gifts. One year I set my heart on a set of two dolls in a cardboard box that had a frill surround in perforated white paper: one doll black, the other one white. I spent (with my friends) hours of my time running up to New Dock Road to look in Poolman's window to see if it was still there. I looked through Poolman's window one day and the dolls were missing. I'm very disappointed. There's nothing else I wanted. Mr. Poolman tells me Santa Claus has collected them. At home we made paperchains out of coloured sheets of paper cut into strips. We also made paper lanterns. Our Christmas tree would be hung with icing clocks and pink mice, pretty paper, chocolate cigars, cardboard stars and everyone had a present. Usually we had a goose dinner with a special afters, trifle. Two different coloured jellies would be available for tea, with a pink blancmange, too. The jelly might be set in a rabbit mould. If you starved all the year it was made up for at Christmas: it was hard saved for effort, with parents usually going without a lot of things in the months from September onwards. On Christmas night we children would go out and visit our friends to see what presents they had and to have a sing-song and share sweets. Our meeting places were usually the garden sheds cleaned out and decorated for the occasion. Most sheds had stone or brick fireplaces so heat was no problem, though smoke might be.[2] On New Year's Day it was a time for rounding all the shops to have a new penny and a stamp on your arm to prevent you from returning a second time. There would be a mile long queue outside Shop Olive for new pennies. Mr. Olive was the town benefactor with two grocery shops. All the children would sing,

Blwyddyn newydd dda i chwi,
Ac i bawb sydd yn y tŷ.
Dyma'r flwyddyn wedi dod,
Y flwyddyn newydda' erio'd. [3]

On New Year's Day in the afternoon, there was a free matinee in the New Dock Cinema with free packets of nuts. We would go to see *The Perils of Pauline.*[4]

Our parents were hospitable. We entertained all our visiting friends and relations. My father's workmates and friends from the Fire Brigade and Docker's Union called in to see us.[5] My mother only protested once when a man and a woman playing the hurdy-gurdy in our street, begged a meal and Dad invited them in. While they were eating they quarrelled with each other, and called one another foul names: we children were all sent out of earshot. It was a prim age we lived in: best leg competitions were judged only as far as the knee—further up would be improper. It was improper to go to church without a hat; it was improper to smoke (for ladies or girls) or drink—that would be scandalous behaviour. Improper to stare at people; to answer back; to accept money for assistance such as window cleaning, walking a baby in a pram, taking care of small children, running errands, and any other

[2] Violet probably means the outhouses used as a laundry, rather than a shed, as such.

[3] "Happy New Year to you, And all within your home. The New Year has come in. The best New Year of all."

[4] *The Perils of Pauline* was a silent serial film in which the daughter of a noted scientist sought a deadly gas formula in Indo-China. Universal Studios brought out a semi-remake in twelve episodes in 1934.

[5] Violet's father was one of the founder members of the South Wales Regional Docker's Union. There was a photograph of the six members hanging in the parlour where he sometimes held meetings.

needed assistance. This was not enforced. It was simply the order of the day. To survive you helped one another. When one of my brothers, Cliff, cut his leg on a broken bottle we sent for Doctor Smith. He had a neighbour, Mrs. Rees, to swing his watch back and forwards before Cliff's eyes while he stitched up the wound, which was cut to the bone. The street heard the screams, my mother fainted, and we all ran out of the house. When our doctor first started his rounds he went everywhere on his bike; later he elevated himself to a motorcycle and sidecar.

My father helped my mother whenever he could, with the washing, the shopping and taking care of us when we were ill, until we grew up to more or less do for ourselves—not forgetting that this was a time when children worked in the mines at fourteen years old. In the summer months our parents would go out to a farm and help bring in the hay, taking us with them. We would spend whole days working in the fields, enjoying rides on the hay cart and a general rough and tumble.

We had great holiday times in August. The summer days saw us preparing in the morning, early, to picnic down on the Bulwarks. This meant carrying quite a lot: sticks, paper, fresh water, kettles, potatoes for fire-roasting, bread loaf and butter. We would take a ball, tennis rackets and shorts in case one fell in the sea and had to change into shorts while crouching in the gorse bushes. Wet clothes were then hung to dry on top of the gorse while the unfortunate one shivered in shorts and blankets. At one time, we went unsupervised to the Bulwarks to play and started to paddle. The ebb tide was very strong with fast undercurrents, and in some places shifting sand. Megan, my sister, started kicking up the water and fell backwards and was borne off with the tide. Fortunately one of the boys grabbed her hair and pulled her ashore. We kept it a secret, otherwise the Bulwarks would have been placed out of bounds.

When the fair came to Llanelli it was a special time. There would be magicians, jugglers, stalls making nougat bars and sideshows. Some years later, when I was a noisy teenager, we sneaked into one of these sideshows. It was supposed to be a naughty one by the look of the poster and the posing, advertising *The Little Bare Behind*: we did—we saw the Little Bear Behind. Fairs were exciting places. The palmist would be busy. There would be a boxing booth.

As teenagers we all took part in the Monkey's Parade in Stepney Street.[6] It was where we met the opposite sex. We would all walk up one side of the street, then down the other. Snobs kept to the right (office workers and other clean hand workers) and riff-raff to the left (factory and other manual workers), each kept to their own side. This Monkey's Parade took place after the church or chapel Sunday night services. It involved one or two turns from one end of Stepney Street to the other: chatting to friends one had not seen all week, and generally keeping in touch. Saturday night's Monkey Parade was different: it took place after the cinemas had spilled out their patrons. It was later. Dancing was coming to the fore then, so it was not unusual to see the girls in their long dance dresses in the parade: they came after the dance was over.

In the late twenties and early thirties, we would travel from village to village to see what kind of dancers there were, and what kind of dance bands and dances. In this way, we teenagers picked up ballroom, jazz, jive and the frowned upon jitter bugging. We danced at the Ritz and Drill Hall, Llanelli, and at the Catholic, Masonic and Church Halls. Earlier flapper girls had gone to Charlie Brown's Speakeasy: it was considered only fast girls went there. Some dances were chaperoned, a girl's parents went with her. But in Charlie Brown's, girls went without chaperones: therefore, it was a fast place. If flappers went there, they did so on the sly. When we wanted a change of scene, we all travelled down to Swansea to the Patti Pavilion for Latin American dancing. At the Mackworth Hotel there were tea dances. In the Elysium Cinema basement there were jazz and jive. We danced at Kidwelly, Burry Port, Bynea, Gorseinon as well as Swansea. We did the rounds. Girls would save up for weeks to buy a dance dress and go to the market to buy one. Lovely beaded dresses could be bought second hand. Some dances were strictly exclusive, by invitation only—the Firemens', the Policemens', various Army Regiments in their do's at their own Drill

[6] These Monkey Parades, as they were called, are mentioned in other towns. The Parade offered young people a regular venue to meet and gossip. It also served to introduce young unattached men and women to each other. If you were attracted to a member of the opposite sex, they said you had 'clicked'.

Hall—you could mingle, dance, and observe the niceties of the day. The women would wear their long organdie dresses, have shoulder flower sprays, wear long gloves, take beaded purses with their compacts and powder puffs.

On leaving school at fourteen, girls could either work in an office or shop for half-a-crown a week, or go into the local factory and make ten or eleven shillings a week. If you went into the factory you had to buy all your protective clothing out of your wages. Boys didn't earn much more, but most of them were on piece-work and by sheer hard work slogged away for more money. I decided to go into the factory and got rigged out in pinafore, coarse apron, headscarf, woollen stockings and clogs. I wanted to make more than half-a-crown a week.

EMILY REES OF TIRCOED FARM, GLANAMAN, CARMARTHENSHIRE

Born February 20th, 1919
Daughter of David Rees and his wife
Gwendoline Rees, née Lewis.

My parents were born and bred in the Aman Valley. My father had been born there in 1887, at Brynaman which was situated at the top end. My mother was born in 1892 at Glanaman, at the lower end of the valley and was five years younger than my father: he had one sister. My paternal grandfather was a miner working in the local colliery, but my mother was one of a large family, consisting of seven girls and three boys.[1] Her father was Lewis Lewis who was a tin worker in the Glanaman tin works, but he also rented a smallholding called Tircoed Farm, situated above the village, which was part of the Dynevor estate which was made up of many farms and smallholdings in that part of Carmarthenshire.

I can recall as a child that Lord and Lady Dynevor would visit the farm at Tircoed once a year to collect the rent: they made a personal visit. It was an occasion for great preparation; everything had to be in its proper order for the Lord and Lady's annual inspection. We would all be assembled to greet them. My grandfather had a great respect for Lord Dynevor, who he considered to be a very fair man in relation to his tenants. They would go round to all their tenants for the rent money. One thing I remember clearly, and that's her Ladyship's clothes. Lady Dynevor wore heavy dark stockings which had been darned. It struck me as very odd that a rich lady would wear stockings that had been worn until they had holes in them and had to be darned.

Now it so happened that my maternal grandmother died young, leaving a widower with a large family, ten of them in all. Sometime later my grandfather re-married a distant relation of his, a widow, who had three young daughters of her own.[2] When she moved in the

---

[1] Their names were Lizzie, May, Gwendoline, Sarah Ellen, May, Berta and Maggie Olwen. The boys were David John, William Ewart and Gwyn.

[2] Ollie, Mariel and Lizzie.

153

farmhouse was bursting at the seams: there were only four bedrooms, three large and one box-room (very small) to accommodate my grandfather, his new wife, and thirteen children of varying ages. As you can imagine, friction was inevitable. My step-grandmother was devoid of any affection. A hard woman, she showed no emotion towards her own daughters and even less for her seven step-daughters. Despite this, and probably because of my step-grandmother's very harsh treatment, my mother would often tell me that as a girl her sisters and step-sisters all united in their dislike of this unfeeling woman, and got on reasonably well.

Because of this terrible overcrowding at Tircoed, the older sisters married young and left the farm: it was a means of getting out of an unbearable home life. It was during this time, as a teenager, that my mother met this very handsome young man called David Rees: he was over six feet tall, blond, with piercing deep blue eyes. He cut quite a figure. At the age of twenty-one when she met him, he was already an overman in the colliery. Being ambitious, he wanted to get on, and so he decided that the best thing to do was to emigrate to America, leave Wales for the mining areas of Pennsylvania.

In 1908 my father-to-be left for the States. He soon established himself in a place called Easton, and it was then that he sent for my mother. She was just eighteen; she had waited two years, and was now ready to cross the Atlantic on her own and marry him in Pennsylvania. Although she must have wondered what was waiting for her in a place like America, it was probably going to be a lot better than the conditions at Tircoed.

My mother was married five years before she gave birth to her first child, a son named Frances Howard, born in 1915. Then, two years later she had another child, but it died. I was born in 1919 and my birth certificate shows that my father was already a member of the Canadian armed forces, having enlisted some time during the First World War. With her husband away in the army, my mother had taken lodgings with a German family in Easton: they were the Mertz family. There was my father away fighting the Germans, while we lived happily with a German family in Pennsylvania. They had four sons who spoiled me terribly. Mrs. Mertz was extremely kind to my mother, who had finally come to realize that her husband had no intention of coming back to America.

There had been problems in my parent's marriage during the birth of my brother and I. My father, apparently, had a drink problem. Although he could obtain good positions in the colliery, he always lost them after going for periods of heavy drinking: a drinking bout. Then he would lose time, and eventually the management would dismiss him. After our father went off to Canada to enlist, Mrs. Mertz looked after my brother and I while our mother worked in a munitions factory. After the war ended, my mother eventually learned that our father had been demobilised in Canada and had then returned to his home in Wales. All her fears had proved right.

My mother was left with all the memories of a young Welsh girl of just eighteen, arriving at Ellis Island full of high hopes and aspirations for the future. She would tell us about the sea voyage, and about meeting up with her fiancée. Ellis Island was a formidable place: every immigrant had to pass through it. There were so many young women, like herself, from all over the world, arriving to marry their men. All these young women had to undergo very stringent vetting: which included a strict medical examination. Our mother would tell us about the many sad scenes when some of the women were discovered as having contracted tuberculosis, or, perhaps, some sexually transmitted disease. This barred them from entry to America and so they were refused entry. They were compelled to remain on Ellis Island until such time as a passage back to their own country could be arranged. These women were desolate when having to part from their men and return home. There were heart-breaking scenes.

During the years from my birth in 1919 until 1922, my mother had learned from letters from my grandfather that my own father had returned to his mother in Brynaman. My grandfather now wrote insisting that my mother, with her children, return and take up residence with him and my step-grandmother at Tircoed Farm. However, as there was no possibility of any reconciliation between my mother and father, my mother (who was a very strong-minded and independent character) had decided that she could not face the humiliation of going back to her small Welsh village and the gossip that would be stirred up: she had decided to stay in America and bring up her children alone.

Letters continued to come to us from Tircoed. My mother learned that my father had had his passage to South Africa paid for by his mother, and that he had gone out there to look for work. But for some reason, due to his drinking problem, he had been deported and was back in Wales. Apart from the humiliation and shame of returning to Glanaman having been deserted in America by her husband, my mother dreaded the thought of having to live under the same roof as her step-mother with her children: the thought horrified and distressed her. She thought when she had left at eighteen that she was going for good, or at least until her husband had accumulated sufficient wealth to return some day to Wales and re-establish the family in a home of their own. Until that time we had only ever lived in part of someone else's home: she had never had a house she could call her own. Although our mother had been determined to stay and make ends meet in the States, it all got too much for her. Eventually, my mother succumbed to the many requests from my grandfather to return home to Tircoed. When one of the letters she received included enough money to pay for the ship's passage for the three of us, she could not hold out any longer. The money represented tickets that she could never have afforded to buy herself: so she settled on returning to Wales.[3]

At the age of four, or five, I arrived in the Aman Valley: an American kid. My earliest recollections are of being surrounded by so many adults, all talking a foreign language—Welsh—which we had not been taught, although I suppose my mother and father would have retained and spoken Welsh together in America. My brother and I were a great source of amusement to the other members of the family: these included my mother's step-sisters and her younger brother, also a half-brother, the precious one, our grandfather's and step-grandmother's only child.

I was fascinated by the farm and the animals, always dragging my brother out to explore with me. We were the "little Yanks." I never called my brother by his real name, only Bud or Buddy. We children

[3] Most of what I write about these years I learned from my mother as an adult; as I was only four or five at the time.

had no idea what our mother's feelings were on returning to the farm: it held no happy memories for her. And now she was virtually a servant in her father's house: a skivvy. Her step-mother continually humiliated her over her broken marriage, always taunting her about her inability to hold her husband. She always blamed my mother for the break-up of the marriage, although she was fully aware of the circumstances surrounding the break-up due to my father's behaviour: his bad drinking habits.

Step-grandmother's pride and joy was her son: we soon discovered that. She never tried to disguise her favouritism towards him. We were never allowed, or given, fresh fruit, but we knew that my step-grandmother had apples, oranges and bananas locked in the large pantry. We could smell the fruit, my brother and I, but it was only her son that ate them out of our sight. All these different things hurt us.

It could be said step-grandmother was thrifty. She would collect eggs and lock them away in the pantry until she had sufficient to take them down to the local Co-op branch in the village to sell. Likewise, she would make butter from the cream of the milk to sell; but let us go back to the eggs: like the fruit, these were *not* for our consumption. That is, not hen eggs. My brother and I had to share the much larger duck egg, while her son had his own hen's egg. She always wore long black skirts with a large black apron, which had deep pockets inside the apron. I had seen her going around collecting the eggs and noted that, once she had collected a number of eggs in her apron pockets, she had to walk slow and deliberate to avoid the eggs smashing against each other. One day, I waited until she had collected a large number of eggs and then I saw my chance and ran forward calling out "Grammy, come and see," and at the same time I pressed both hands hard on her apron, resulting in a yellow stream of egg yolk trickling from her apron. It was quite deliberate on my part: which she knew. But, although she was very angry, she could not punish me for something I pretended had been an accident.

Of course, by now I had started to attend the village school where all lessons were in Welsh, which presented its own problems. My brother and I were regarded as being odd because of our American accents: we were teased because of it. I also had another problem, because of being born with weak ankles, the doctor in America advised my mother that I would always have to wear boots that came over the ankles; they were ugly and cumbersome, and I came in for a lot of teasing from the other children because they wore shoes.

There was truancy among children at Glanaman Primary School; generally, they were from the larger and poorer families in the village. The children were kept from school by their parents because the child had worn out his shoes and they could not afford to buy new ones— perhaps. If a child had not attended school for some time and the teacher or headmaster had no word from the parents as to why the child was not in attendance—a man in uniform, the Attendance Officer or "Whipper-in", as he was known, would call on the parents and warn them of the consequences: if the child was ill it was a different matter. Glanaman school had no kitchen, so our cookery lesson took place in the adjoining village of Garnant, in the primary school which was bigger and had a kitchen. We had to walk about a mile or so to Garnant which made the lesson last all afternoon. We only made cakes or scones, anything else was out of the question because we had to walk back home carrying the cakes. Sewing lesson was mainly simple embroidery on a handkerchief or tablecloth and napkins, nothing more.

My days on the farm were idyllic, but my school days were hateful. My brother was much quicker at learning than I was: which made him quite popular with the teachers, while I, being so much slower, and not very interested, was not. There was one teacher who was particularly taken by my brother who showed an intense dislike of me, the feeling was mutual: I positively hated her.

The living conditions at the farm were still overcrowded. My step-grandmother's three daughters were still there, my mother's two younger sisters were still at home, as were my brother and I and my mother's youngest brother Gwyn, and my mother's half-brother who was about the same age as my brother: so there were eleven of us. And our mother did so much of the work. Monday was wash day: which was done in the large kitchen that had a flagged floor and an enormous scrubbed-top table. Water came from a mountain stream from which my grandfather had formed a dam: from this he ran pipes (the dam being some yards up the hill) to a point in the farmyard where all the water ran into a wooden tub: when it was full the water just overflowed into a ditch which diverted to the stream lower down the hill. We used to wash in that tub summer and winter. We used to call it in Welsh—*y pistyll*.

For wash day the water was carried in small milk carriers from the tub into the kitchen and then poured into a large container on the open brick fire. A tub was placed on two kitchen chairs and the washing was done in this tub; nearby there would be two bowls on the table: one contained Reckitts blue (or dolly blue), a small bag of blue powder soaking in the bowl, and then bleach in the other bowl—for a whiter wash. Washing took all morning. I was always in school, so didn't get involved in it. Ironing was done with heavy flat irons heated on the fire, using two irons: while one was in use, the other was on the fire. To test the iron to see if it was hot enough, they would spit on the flat surface. If the spit flew off the surface it was hot enough: not very hygienic.

My grandfather, who I regarded as my father, was a rather fierce looking man, rather large, with a drooping walrus moustache. He was well respected in the community and a senior deacon of the Calvinistic Methodist Chapel. He attended chapel regularly and all the members of the family had to attend: morning service, Sunday School, and evening service. Visiting ministers would always stay with us: they would say that they were well fed with Lewis Lewis and his brood at Tircoed. Mind, I never ever remember my mother attending chapel when I was small. She was always left behind, like a servant, to do the cooking, cleaning and attending the animals or working in the fields. Ollie, Mariel and Lizzie, my mother's step-sisters were all academics, in spite of their own mother being only semi-literate. One had taken teacher-training and was teaching; another was attending ladies college, but Ollie had become ill with tuberculosis and spent a lot of time in hospital, and long periods of illness at home.

It was with this sick aunt, Ollie, that I spent much of the long winter nights: being amused by her. I also slept with the three sisters. Ollie eventually died. She was only nineteen. And that was my first experience of bereavement. Ollie's coffin lay in the tiny parlour at the farm. I can remember the coffin being carried out to the farmyard by these men, and then all the men proceeded to the cemetery on the mountain. The men took turns to carry the coffin. Within a few years, the other two sisters died of tuberculosis too: all so very young. It appeared to me at the time that the adults around me accepted death, even in the young, as a kind of fate that one could not avoid. And in this acceptance of death, grief was pointless: it had happened. Mourning was also not apparent. The people were practical and life had to go on. So mourning was not evident. The passing of the three sisters depleted this large family somewhat. There was more room to breathe. My mother's sisters, Tydfil and Berta, had also married and left the farm, which now left only seven of us.[4]

My grandfather was my champion always. I would tease my brother and step-uncle until they retaliated, and when they did I would run calling "Grampa! Grampa!" And my grandfather would come running (as much as he could run because of his arthritis), wielding his stick and shouting at them in Welsh. My brother and I were both Welsh speaking by this time and fully integrated into the life of the school and, of course, the chapel. My step-grandmother continued to persecute my mother, which I became more aware of as I got older. My mother was being punished for having a husband who had run off and abandoned her with two small children. Every day there would be snide remarks: it all must have been very hurtful. I wonder if she ever bitterly regretted coming back to Tircoed. She must have been unhappy. But what I can say of my own childhood is, that it was happy. We were well fed and my step-grandmother insisted that my mother bought the best of clothes. This was not due to her generosity; it had more to do with her pride. Nobody would be able to point a finger at a member of the Tircoed family and say we were shabby.

My mother had started to earn some money of her own as we were growing up: this was something she had not been able to do up until then. She worked full-time for her step-mother and father, morning, noon and night, for the roof over our heads and the food and for the clothing we wore. The money she earned was by going to neighbours'

---

[4] My mother, my brother and I, my mother's youngest brother Gwyn (whom I idolised), my mother's half-brother, and, of course, grandfather and step-grandmother.

houses to decorate a room for 2s.6d. I would often go with her to watch her skill at hanging wallpaper. It gave her a little independence. Not much.

My brother and I were growing up by now: I was a teenager, not academically inclined, while my brother did apply himself rather well. My mother's brother Gwyn had attended Grammar school, and later qualified as an architect and surveyor and had married. My mother's half-brother had also passed to Grammar school, attended and obtained his degree at Aberystwyth University, become a teacher and later headmaster of Ystalyfera Grammar School. My brother left school at fourteen and went to work with my Uncle Gwyn, my mother's brother, who had established his own practice in surveying for rural councils in Carmarthenshire and Pembrokeshire, working on rural water and sewerage schemes.

Eventually my grandfather moved out of the farm with his wife, to a small house in the village. And my mother's brother with his wife and family took over the tenancy of the farm. My mother just stayed on with him and his family, helping with the children, and, of course, now helping her brother on the farm. She just "went with the farm," working as hard as ever.

At fourteen I, too, left school. My Auntie Sal had a job as a waitress at The Seabank Hotel, the largest hotel on the seafront at Porthcawl, and she arranged for me to join her there. Staff slept three to a room, which was quite big: it had a double bed and a single bed, a wardrobe and dressing table. I shared the double bed with Auntie Sal (my mother's sister). There were separate staff toilets, bathroom and a staff room. We all had breakfast at 7.30 a.m., usually sausage and bacon cooked by the chef. The chef was a Frenchman, and very temperamental: nobody was allowed in the kitchen. I remember one occasion when the manager went in the kitchen to complain about something, and the chef chased him out of the kitchen wielding a large carving knife. We nearly all went on strike over that.

My training began by laying tables in the staff room and serving the office staff: then I graduated to a "commie" waitress, helping a waitress in the diners' restaurant, and clearing tables. My wage was five shillings a week and it cost four shillings and sixpence bus fare to go home on my half-day: so I was only sixpence in pocket. I was asked to help the store keeper one day, and she told me to clean the bread cutting machine, and I had an accident with it and cut the top of my finger— about one inch of my finger was severed through to the bone, and only hung on by skin. A doctor came and sewed my finger together again under chloroform in the hotel. I did not work for six months after that, but funnily enough, I was paid sick benefit of seven shillings and sixpence a week, instead of my normal five shillings a week for all that work: on duty at 8a.m., work through until 2p.m.—then two hours off—start again at 4p.m. sharp, until 8p.m., with one half-day off a week. All the staff had to be back in the hotel by 10p.m. every night. It was 1933 and a waitress like me did all those hours for five shillings. And remember, if I went back to Tircoed to see my mother[5], it left me with sixpence a week.

[5] Emily's mother eventually obtained the position of cook in the Glanaman Colliery Canteen, and later became Matron of Pibwrlwyd Farm Institute for male, and later female, students at Carmarthen. She died in Glanaman in 1974 aged eighty-four years.

MILDRED EVANS OF PEN-Y-GRAIG, NEAR TONYPANDY

Born November 26th, 1920
Daughter of Evan Evans and his wife
Catherine Evans née Jenkins

My mother was born in 1876, and when she was old enough she was sent to a big house in Pen-y-graig to be a housemaid. Dad was a year older than she and worked on his father's farm outside Builth Wells. It was called Letty Cottage Farm. Eventually he left to find work in Pen-y-graig, and that's where he met our mother. She was eighteen when she married. You were considered an old maid if you left it any later. Their courtship would be walking the country lanes; courting couples walked miles in those days.

Mam had eleven children, but lost one at six months, her name was Iris. She buried another daughter too, Gertrude, who died of pneumonia when she was only six. The other death was my brother William when he was twenty-three. There was an old saying in Wales, a superstition, that if you had your photograph taken as an engaged couple, together, one would die: something terrible would happen. There can't be many photographs of engaged couples in family albums. As it happened, my brother died after having such a photo' taken with his fiancée. He was the eldest son and his fiancée was a nurse. William died of pneumonia before I was born. I think he had gone out without a coat on, and came back home soaking wet and got a chill which turned to pneumonia. Mam took his death badly as he was her first born. That was two children who died of pneumonia before I was born. I was the youngest child, the last one, the baby of the family: Mam was fifty-four when she had me.

I was five when I went to Craig-yr-Eos School, built right at the bottom of the mountain in Pen-y-graig. It was a pleasant school. A favourite teacher of mine was a little old maid, well that's the sort of teacher we had, and there was a lot of singing of songs and dancing. Then at six or seven you started learning things. You became more aware of the headmistress as you got older: now she *was* strict. There was the cane for us if we misbehaved. She had a long thin cane, a real stinger: it was her job to give it to us. You would go to her room for punishment, sloping your hand downwards, hoping the blow would slide off. But she was too cunning for that. She pushed your hand up straight with the cane before coming down hard. Some of us used to put a hair across the palm as we thought it blunted the blow. Once I was sitting alongside a friend when a mistress, who was using the board pointer (it was thick one end, then went to a thin point) brought it down sharp across the girl's hand next to mine. She was thought to be misbehaving. Well, it caught my hand too, and gave me a nasty wheal across my knuckles. My father went up to school and threatened them: he was not going to stand for that.

My schooldays were happy. For the girls there was sewing and cooking. Once a week we had to take the ingredients in and we made rice puddings, bread 'n butter pudding and toad in the hole. It gave you a good feeling to take them home for tea. We had outings. You had to save up for them. One outing was a trip to Stratford-upon-Avon, but Mam couldn't afford the five shillings and I was really peeved about this. The day before someone dropped out and the teacher asked if there was anyone who would fill her place. Up my hand went. They sent me to run home. I ran all the way to ask Mam. There she was scrubbing at the washboard, all steamed up, and when I told her what I wanted she said that I should not have put my hand up. I suppose I looked so crestfallen, that she dried her hands and got the rent money—which was exactly five shillings—and gave it to me. Dad was mad when he found out. The day we went it poured with rain and I wasn't interested in Shakespeare. It was a most disappointing day. And the rent money had been spent.

We lived in a rented terrace house, owned by a landlord. Three bedrooms upstairs, two rooms downstairs (a front room and a kitchen) a lavatory outside and no bathroom. All the houses were neglected. All the owner was interested in were the rents. They were a bit run-down. Stone houses in a terrace. They would have been bought as a package: if you bought one you had to buy the lot. The rent collector came round on a Monday, usually in the evening. Everybody came on a Monday: the rent collector, the tally-man (for borrowed money, for the payments on clothes bought on the never-never) and the insurance man. We all had death insurances to make sure there were decent burials. All these men called on a Monday, at the beginning of the week to make sure you still had some money. Wages were collected by the men on Saturday afternoon—even if you had finished your shift on a Friday you still had to wait—all the miners got paid then. These people wouldn't collect on a Sunday, so Monday was their day. Dad would dole out the various bits of money to Mam on Saturday. The men ruled the house. Do not forget it. No woman got the wage packet intact. That scene in the film *How Green Was My Valley* all about a Welsh mining village has a scene in it where the Mam holds out her apron and all the men of the family put their wage packets in it, nicely, well that is all wrong. It is pure Hollywood. There wasn't a woman in Pen-y-graig, not in Tonypandy, that got a man's wage packet given to her. That scene is not showing what really happened. The first thing the men did when they got the wage packet was go to the pub. Half of it was spent there, in the pub, before they even got home. Our Dad and most of the men did it. Spent the afternoon in the pub. Mam would have the tea ready for him hours before he finally got home. What was left of the pay packet was then doled out to her: what *he* thought she ought to have. Don't think that she ever had any *say* in the matter. Money was tight. Mam didn't have much to spare: that's why it was wonderful of her to let me go to Stratford on the school trip.

Medical attention was expensive. Medicines were expensive. So most women had some sort of concoction they could make up. Goose grease came in handy: it could be put on a sock, with the foot part wrapped around the neck for a sore throat. Warm goose grease rubbed all over your chest to bring up the phlegm: the smell was horrible. We children would be sent out to collect dandelions and burdock; it was soaked in water and became a horrible khaki colour: this was taken for acne. My complexion was good so I didn't have to drink it. We made our own sulphur tablets with lard and sulphur: taken to purify the blood. Everybody used these concoctions because medicines had to be paid for. When someone died, a local woman, a neighbour, came to lay out the dead. In Tonypandy though, midwives *did* lay out the dead. Most families tried to get a neighbour to do it because the woman only charged a few shillings. But if a neighbour could not be found to do this, then they sent for the midwife:: but she charged more. It was the midwife who was the professional layer-out.

My father worked hard down the mine. He would come home covered in coal dust: it got in their eyes, too. My father cleaned the coal dust out of his eyes with the corner of the towel twisted into a point: he would spit on it and then wipe out the dust. That's how they kept their eyes free of dust, with nothing caught in the corners. Most miners paid in fourpence a week for a doctor: to be able to go to the doctor when they were ill. Our Dad regularly coughed up coal dust: he eventually died of silicosis. All the doctors were pro-colliery owners and did what they were told. Dad died of silicosis, but the doctor wrote down on the death certificate: pneumonia. That was so that Mam would not be able to claim compensation from the colliery. It was useless to contest it. A waste of time. The colliery owners were not going to give compensation payments to the widows of miners: it would all mount up.

About the age of six or so, it was my job to wash my father's back when he came home from the mine. Also the backs of my four brothers: five backs in all. Mam had the water all ready boiling away; it was kept hot on the fire in an oval cast iron boiler. We had a beer cask cut in half, which held about eight or nine gallons of water. A beer cask cut down made a handy bath, but it was so heavy: it was rolled into place before the fire. When not in use it was kept on its side in the back yard. There were more tubs like this around than zinc baths. The handles were made out of the wood of the barrel. There I would be waiting for them to come in. Mam poured the water into the wooden cask. Dad was washed first if the brothers and he were on the same shift. There were three shifts, and so, if they were on different ones, Mam and I did it three separate times: except, if it was a night shift Mam did it all.

With the water nice and hot, Dad knelt down and washed his face and arms, while I washed his back. After that, I went to wait outside until he had finished inside the bath. Then a brother was washed. I did his back in the same way. After all the men had washed, their clothes were shaken free of coal dust out in the back yard. This shaking also got rid of all the black beetles in their clothes, quite big ones, long ones. They lived in the timbers down in the mines and were about an inch long: some were dark red and we called them *Red Indians*. The men's vests, pants and socks were then put in the bath water afterwards, to have a soak. Mam washed them all out straightaway, then hung them up on the rail in the kitchen or on the big fireguard.

It seems as if our kitchen was always full of drying clothes. If it was a weekend, or the weather was fine, we put the wet clothes out in the garden to dry. A miner's wife needed a mangle: it was essential. A mangle wasn't only used for clothes. Rhubarb could be put through it for wine-making, and parsnips, too, to get the juice out. Mam would turn the handle and I would feed the rhubarb through the rollers. Wine was made regularly in our house: it was for medicinal purposes. We made a lot of elderflower wine; a red hot poker was plunged into a glass of elderflower wine to warm the drink, and then taken out and a bit of sweetening added. My father always seemed to have colds. The warm wine was good for them.

Women never went to pubs, only to the jug and bottle (an off-licence which was part of the public house). Mam never went drinking. She had seen enough of what booze did. She was a church-goer, and anyway, a woman would get a bad name in the neighbourhood if she went out to the jug and bottle of an evening. It was bad enough with the men drinking their wages away without the women joining in. What would families have done if both parents drank? A disaster. But she did belong to the Womens' Cooperative League and went to their meetings every week. There was also a craze for spiritualist meetings, with seances going on. A lot of women took to spiritualism. It was very popular at the time. It filled some sort of need in the women.

We were all right for coal. There was a concession for miners delivered by a lorry and tipped out at the front door. If Dad wasn't at home, Mam and the children would have to carry it through the house into the back yard. The way we did it was to carry through the big pieces first; we built up a wall with these larger lumps of coal, and after that put the small coal inside: it was then all contained and a tarpaulin was put over it to keep it dry. We didn't have a coal house. If a miner wanted to, he'd build a coal house, but our Dad didn't do this. Some miners' families put their coal under the staircase, called a *cutch*, but it collected black beetles. We would say if someone was hiding, he was *cutching* somewhere. Mam used a sack over her apron when she was stacking the coal. It was made up properly from hessian into the shape of an apron: this covered her clean white apron. She wore the hessian one for stacking the coal or scrubbing the floors. Our house was stone-floored throughout, with only a bit of lino in the front room. There was always a lot of scrubbing going on.

In every home the fire was precious. It had to be kept going all of the time, even in summer. Without it there was no hot water. You wouldn't waste coal even if you lived in a coal village, with your Dad a miner. Every six months you got a delivery of coal—not free, don't think that—you had to pay for it. But it was horrible coal: all the rejected bits separated from the best coal which could not be sold elsewhere. The miners got all the coal that was considered slag, all that was thrown to one side when the quality controller was checking it: that's what we got, *slag*. Half of the delivery was half-coal, more like dust than anything else. The slag burned like a series of layers, like a burned book. If you raked it, it all disintegrated into dust: that's how poor it was. The grates would burn anything as there was always a draught running through the house and the chimney would draw well. At night, just before the last one went to bed the fire was balked up with small coal, the dust, which had previously been dampened with water in the bucket, and then thrown onto the larger coals. This covered the fire like a blanket: it was safe and burned away all night, slowly. It was all ready then, for the morning when it was raked at the bottom and got ready for the day. It was a ritual. The state of the fire depended on what you were cooking that day. If cooking pies, you needed a red fire for the heat. Our fire was more or less continually on, even in the summer. It was regularly raked and the coke was re-used. The whole family depended on that fire being kept going. In 1926, in the General Strike, all my brothers went out to the tip to scrape for coal. A family had to get something to burn, somehow.

When the General Strike came in 1926 I was only six. Dad was out on strike with the others. My brothers went to the soup kitchen to get something to eat: you had to take your own basin. My brothers hated going, they felt humiliated, that it was charity. My brothers were the only ones to go in our family: all you had was a bowl of soup. At the schools you could be issued with a boot chit for free boots. A society, like the Quakers, I believe, came down to Tonypandy and organised a fund to buy boots for miners' children. My Mam applied for a chit for me. It had to be taken to one of the local shops. When she took me along I cried bitterly because I thought that I could only get boots, which I didn't want. The chit was for boots only. But the shop owner took pity on me. I cried so much he relented and gave me lace-up shoes. Just what I wanted.

When I was a child the only place to go was Band-of-Hope to watch the magic lantern shows. It was the only form of entertainment. Somewhere for us to go out of the house. Then when I got to about nine, Mam started to give me a penny to go to the Saturday Matinee show at the pictures. But I had to earn it by cleaning all the brass. Unless you had a sweetheart at school, then he might give you the penny to go. The picture-house in Tonypandy wasn't very grand. For the matinee you would go to your seat to the crunch, crunch of shells: monkey-nuts—peanuts—eaten, with the shells thrown down on the floor. Every Saturday afternoon children would be admitted without their parents, but not in the evening when it was more sedate. You had to be with your parents in the evening, so the place was quieter—they had cleaned up the nut shells too—so it wasn't crunch, crunch, as you moved your feet. It was silent films when we were children, with Charlie Chaplin and that po-faced bloke Buster Keaton. The first talkie I ever saw had Al Jolson in it.

We all flocked to the pictures. My brothers had curly hair, but they were desperate to look like Rudolf Valentino. So they would buy jars of vaseline and plaster it on, all over their head, to make the hair look straight. But Mam complained bitterly about the state of their pillows: that vaseline made a terrible mess when they went to bed. When I was a young girl going to the pictures, there was Norma Shearer: she *was* lovely. I didn't want to be a Garbo, but Norma Shearer. Oh! I wanted to be like her in appearance. That was what we wanted to look like as girls: it wasn't their way of living we wanted, it was their looks. It was hair-styles and make-up. Mind, my parents didn't allow make-up, not before the age of eighteen: it was strictly forbidden. So you would put it on after leaving the house and then wipe it all off before you got back home again. Dad *never* went to the cinema, never, and he never saw anything on stage. It was only the Conservative Club for him: that's where he went to drink.

Dad never talked politics at home. Men didn't discuss such things with their wives: but he was well into it. He was the right hand man of Gwilym Rowlands who was the Conservative M.P. for Mid-Rhondda. There he was, a *miner*, and a staunch Conservative. Dad would get out his black suit and bowler hat, stinking of mothballs, to smarten himself up to go out with Gwilym to a meeting. It was also his funeral suit. When he'd finished with it, back it would go, all folded up, back into the bottom drawer, all wrapped up carefully in tissue paper and mothballs. It was never hung up. Nobody had wardrobes in their bedrooms in those days; it was chests of drawers: that's what we had to keep our clothes in. Nothing was hung up on clothes hangers. What you didn't wear was folded away in a drawer.

I would not have wanted my Mam's life. The women were all so brow-beaten by the men. The man was boss. My grandmother was cowed into silence. She hardly ever spoke. Grandad was the *boss*. Men had the voices. Mam had no opinions of her own, and if she *did*, it wasn't acknowledged: it was as if she had no influence whatsoever. Dad was boss and the wage packet was his to do what he pleased with. He worked hard as a miner and thought he deserved it. He took his drink money out and if he went into the pub on his way home he'd spend what he wanted, then give her the bit that was left. Mam didn't have the same amount each week: it was what he thought fit to give her and his beer money came first. She had to manage on what was left: feed us all on the remains. Mam would buy a sheep's head, say for fourpence, depending on the size. We would eat the brains, the tongue, then the cheeks. What was left was used to make a stew of vegetables, with leeks and carrots. This way the sheep's head would be made to last us about three days: that was good going for fourpence. The pig is good value: there's brawn that can be made, tripe, chitterlings, you eat all of a pig. Mam tried her utmost to keep us all fed on whatever she might get from Dad.

In the right season we would go up the mountain to search for whimberries. Up we would go with our jam jars: they had a bit of string around the neck to make a little handle. We would make a day of it and take some sandwiches and a bottle of lemonade—well, sherbet really, with a bit of water in it—and we would came back with our jars filled with whimberries. Mam would make a tart for Sunday: all done on a Saturday, of course. All the things that could be cooked the day before the Sabbath would be got ready: Mam worked hard on a Saturday to get everything straight for Sunday.

In the sense of her personality, Mam was tolerant (I suppose she had to be) and really the mainstay of our family. We would all go to her if we wanted something, anything, not to Dad: he wouldn't have the time. Dad tended to be cruel anyway: handy with the strap he was. He'd beat my brothers. They would have great wheals on their backs for truanting from school, or going up to the feeder to swim, up the mountain, that wasn't allowed. Or they'd get a hiding for smoking in the *brachis* run by the local Italians: a shop that sold ice-creams, sweets and had a one-armed bandit in it. It was a gathering place for the boys, young men. No girl ever went to the *brachi* to socialize. Perhaps a girl would pop in to buy an ice-cream, but never to hang around in: no girl would loiter in the *brachi*: it was the boys' world, in there. It wasn't the place for girls. The only place for girls was something Christian, something run by the Sunday School, Band-of-Hope, Christian Endeavour or Girl Guides. The *brachi* was definitely out of bounds for young girls, teenagers; you would be considered a terrible *tart* if you hung around a *brachi*. No decent girl would risk being called a tart.

Sex was a word we never even heard. It was a taboo subject and a taboo word. Nobody ever said it. At school they gave us lessons on childbirth. Not that we knew very much. The lesson would be given by a visitor, a visiting teacher and we would all be none the wiser after listening to it: it remained a mystery. This visitor came twice a year to speak to us girls: it was the eleven year olds who would start to hear the talks. Another visitor, was Nitty Nora, who came regularly to look for nits. If you *did* have nits you were made to have your head all shaved, which was a terrible shaming thing to do to a child.

At fourteen it was time for me to leave school and so we started to look around for jobs. Dad was willing to pay for me to train as a hairdresser. We needed about ten pounds for the training, apprenticeship it was. But I knew it would be a great sacrifice for them as it was a lot of money in 1934. Really, they couldn't afford it. So I said I would rather do something else. We looked in the local newspaper ads for a job in domestic service. That was what most of the girls did. Going into service was about all there was. We found an ad for a job in Breconshire. The woman came down to our house in Pen-y-graig to interview me.

This prospective employer was a huge woman, big, the wife of the rector of Crickhowell. The first thing she says to me is, "And what is your religion?"

Of course, I said Church of England. So the next thing she wanted was to be taken to see our vicar. She wanted to speak to him personally about me. We both got into her car, a little Austin, and drove around to the vicarage. Naturally, I got out of the car and walked up the drive to the door with her. The vicar himself answered the door and greeted me friendly-like, with "Hullo Mildred." I told him that this woman wanted a character reference. Our vicar wanted me to go into the vicarage with her, but she turned quickly and shut the door in my face, wouldn't let me go in. I was stunned. Upset really. It was so nasty of her. The vicar told my mother later that he thought she wouldn't make a kind mistress. Fancy shutting the front door in the face of a fourteen-year-old, leaving me standing there outside.

This rector's wife turned out to be a real devil. A nasty bit of goods she was. And it didn't take long for me to find out as their *tweeny*: a between maid, helping the cook and the housemaid. At the rectory was a cook, a housemaid and a parlour-maid and me: four servants. I was terribly homesick. Had never been away from home before. But this wasn't taken into consideration. They weren't considerate. The rector said I had to go to church on a Sunday, but instead of going into the service, I used to wander around the tombstones, crying my eyes out. I was so unhappy. As a result of my disobedience, the rector's wife would call me up to her bedroom and give me a dressing down for not going into the church service. After she had shouted at me she would give me extra duties as a punishment. After I had been there about six months, my father came up with an uncle in a motorbike and sidecar: on a day's visit to see how I was getting on. I told Dad all about it and said I was unhappy. So Dad said "Hand in your notice girl" and when I went in to tell her, she wouldn't have it: refused to accept it. She didn't want the bother of replacing me.

Another thing which kept me in a nervous state of apprehension was their son, a cadet. The other maids had told me that the son had been found in the previous *tweeny's* bedroom and I had taken her place when she had been dismissed. There was no lock on my bedroom door and so, no way of locking it at night when I went to bed. And so I was petrified when the young man was at home, terrified that he would come into my bedroom: it was at the top of the house, far away from the family. I felt isolated up there.

Dad stuck by my intention to have my notice accepted, although she did not like it. My notice was again handed in and my father wrote her a letter to reinforce it, to get it across to her. She did *not* like this and she insisted that he had written her a rude letter. She sent me away immediately with a month's wages: £1.16s.4d. That was what I got a month for a day that started at 6.30 a.m. (7 at the latest) and which lasted until 9 o'clock at night, with one day a month off, and Sunday afternoon—but you had to go to the church service, so it wasn't really time off—and there was something to slave over all day. She was vindictive to the end and sent me away without a reference: she refused to give me one, knowing that it would be well nigh impossible to get another position without one. That was the sort of devil she was.

Home I went, still only fourteen, and started to look in the newspapers again. This time we found a place which looked promising: with a mine-owner's daughter in Buckinghamshire, Gerrard's Cross, a big country house. It meant leaving Wales, but then, so many girls like me had to in order to get a job. We got over the reference problem by asking the vicar and the headmistress of my school to supply them. My bags were packed and arrangements made by letter for me to go up to London by train. What an adventure that was. I was told to wait at Paddington Station, and wear a white carnation. There I would be met by the family chauffeur who would also be wearing a white carnation: it was all carefully thought out. I got off the train and waited, eventually a man came up to me looking like Boris Karloff: he terrified me. But he *did* have a white carnation and said that the car was in the car park nearby. When we got to it, it was big, with a glass partition, very scary to a young girl. It was getting dark and I started to think that I was being sold into White Slavery. There was a lot of talk of White Slavery: girls being taken by Arabs from Paddington Station, so I worked myself up into a state. There were lots of stories in Tonypandy about White Slavers kidnapping poor girls, unaccompanied, from Paddington Station and the chauffeur's looks didn't help matters. Finally, we reached the big country house and I was taken straight into the drawing-room to meet my new mistress: you weren't allowed to sit down. Not those days. You stood up in front of them.

My new position was under parlour maid, a step up from a *tweeny*. The staff consisted of the chauffeur, a cook, a housemaid, parlour maid and me. I was much happier there. It was much easier. The mistress was kinder: she would even take me in her car down to Wales for a weekend when she was visiting her own family. That was a kindness. We would go down in the chauffeur driven car. I would be dropped off at home, and then collected for the return journey. She didn't send me to sit with the chauffeur in the front, but had me in the back with her: mind, you had to keep your place. But she would talk to me: but no familiarity. *That* would not be permitted.

After two years at Gerrard's Cross I had the urge to better myself. I was now sixteen. So I answered an ad for a parlour maid at a house in East Grinstead: for Lady Margaret Duckworth. I was lucky, and got it. It was even nicer there as Lady Margaret was a dear lady. I would take her tray up to the dining-room; she would eat one course while I sat outside in the hall; then she would ring her bell and I would go in and serve the next course, then out again to wait. She ate on her own, alone in the dining-room. Of course, when she entertained I did it properly and stayed in the dining-room the whole time. Ascot Week was good. I always looked forward to it as the guests all tipped me. I saved money with Lady Margaret. All her servants were happy there. I was not homesick. The treatment I got there was so different from that meted out by the rector's wife. It was a far cry from life at the rectory.

I stayed with Lady Margaret about two years and then left to work

174

for a doctor in Harley Street, but I didn't stay there very long: it was slave labour compared with Lady Margaret's. I had gone as a parlour maid, but ended up as a general dogsbody. After that I jumped from the frying pan into the fire and went to work for another Jewish family, at Stoke Newington. That was another frightening experience: waiting to meet up with my future employer. He came to a pre-arranged place, and turned out to be the ugliest man I had ever seen: really horrible. His nose was flattened. But he turned out to be pleasant enough. At this new place I had to sleep with the children, just looking after them and doing the cleaning for the mistress.

The Stoke Newington place was a different world from the one I had known with Lady Margaret. They weren't wonderful with food. If the family had chicken, for example, they gave me only the neck and the gizzard: it was a shock I can tell you. I was the only one they employed. There was absolutely no privacy: not even my own room. I only stuck it out for four months: that was enough I can tell you. So, I went back home to Tonypandy. My parents didn't mind. I had not been sending them any money and so had a few savings: not much mind. So, on the dole I went. There were many the same way. Then my brother's children came, and so for five years I looked after them.

When the War started in 1939 I went into the munitions factory in Bridgend. We girls used to come home with yellow hands and faces. I painted the shells. But the lead in the paint gave me painter's colic, so I was put in the experimental sheds where we were all locked up in the day and put on special clothing for the job. There were always lots of explosions: my cousin was killed there.

AFTERWORD

Jeffrey Grenfell-Hill has evinced a special interest in social history ever since he was a student and a genuine gift for penetrating to the heart of it. He is an unusually good and interested listener and one with a lively talent for encouraging others to confide in him. In this book he has assembled a fascinating collection of miscellaneously varied recollections of childhood. They were experienced in different parts of Wales, though mostly in the industrial south, during the years from 1895 to 1939. The reader is likely to be struck immediately by what retentive memories the author's respondents have and with what vivid and telling minuteness they can recall those days so long ago. Many of our informants show that remarkable capacity ordinary people possess for breathing life into the scenes they are describing and not being content with just prosily recapitulating events and circumstances. There is that young girl of sixteen, Sarah Bowen, from my own home town of Merthyr, as a maid in London so homesick that she wandered through Paddington station hoping to 'see a face she knew' and being 'quite overcome' when she saw a policeman from home.

The conditions described in the different chapters of the book vary noticeably in detail. While it is the historian's normal practice to generalize from the particular, the circumstances unveiled by the author show the marked disparities that might exist within a comparatively limited area. Some were caused by the subtle gradations from one social class to another, others by the contrasting fortunes which befell families, and still others by the variations in temperament and fortune between individuals. In spite of all these differences, though, there were certain broad characteristics which tended to typify most, if not all, of them.

One cannot but be struck by how much harder life was in general during the first third of the century than it is now. Hours of employment for the men in the mines, the steel, copper and tin works, and on the land, were longer, more exhausting and less well paid. They and their families were vastly more at the mercy of industrial injury, sickness, slump, short time, and unemployment; not to mention being unable to escape from poky, ill-built, overcrowded and inconvenient houses. The womenfolk, poor creatures, fared even worse, especially in working-class families. Ground down by their husbands—'father was always the boss'; exhausted by the demands of regular child-bearing and large families; conscripted to perform the endless round of domestic chores and household labours with never a hint of those labour-saving devices now so blithely taken for granted; they had to struggle desperately, too, to nurse sick members of the family back to health, avoiding as far as humanly possible the need to call on the doctor's unaffordable expense. As one child remembered pathetically, 'I wonder how my mother put up with us all?' In my own recollections of this era, it was the women who were the unsung heroines of the community.

Nor did children have much more of a life of it—how could they in the prevailing circumstances? The reader will quickly be bound to observe just how soon quite young children were called upon to shoulder responsibilities: looking after young brothers or sisters, performing a variety of tasks about the house, having to look for part-time jobs and, in most cases, being obliged to leave school early. Many of them would surely have agreed with that respondent who confessed sadly, ' I had no joy in my childhood.'

Yet children usually contrived to find some routes out of their hardships and discovered outlets for their abundance of mischief and high spirits. One generation of them handed on to the next a wealth of lore concerning a whole series of games and pastimes, which either needed no equipment at all or else devices of the simplest kind like a ball stuffed with rags or a 'catty and dog' (a long stick and a short one). There were also pranks galore which not even the strictest parent wholly succeeded in stifling. Two institutions which provided for children's needs were the schools and chapels. Schools were not universally popular. Some teachers were kind and sympathetic, and children obviously warmed to such unwonted marks of affection. Discipline, however, seems generally to have been strict, even harsh, as I remember from my schooldays, and learning methods were mostly dull and unimaginative. Small wonder, then, that many pupils were not sorry to leave such penitentiaries and escape into the world to earn some money. Chapels played a much larger role in most people's lives than they do nowadays. Children didn't care overmuch for being compelled to attend three services on Sunday and being sternly restrained from playing games on the sabbath. Yet Sunday School and

Band of Hope could be real emancipation in an otherwise monotonous round. As one young girl recalled, 'the only comfort I had in life was going to Band of Hope on Tuesdays, choir practice on Wednesdays, and Christian Endeavour on Fridays.' Whatever else they disliked about chapels, they all revelled in the Sunday School treats. In a world where paid holidays were almost unkown for most, a trip to the neighbouring countryside, or better still, the more distant seashore, was a glimpse of paradise.

For all the off-putting worries and hazards of married existence, most young people were eager to enter into it and leave home. Some endearing reminiscences are brought to mind here of the ways which young men and women devised to find a partner and pair off with one another. There was in almost every community something akin to the 'monkey parade' and the 'bunny run' described in these pages; and though I hadn't heard the term used for ages the mention of 'clicking' brought all the tremulous excitement vividly back to me! For a short while, before the cares of married life closed about these young people, they were able to give expression to all their mutual youthful ardour.

Mr Grenfell-Hill's book was of more than ordinary interest to me. Having lived through about half the period resurrected in its pages, I found myself inevitably comparing and contrasting the recollections of its respondents with those of my own experience. Many were similar, others completely different. But whatever their nature, they brought back in graphic, atmospheric detail for me, a world that I had once lived in. For many other people I've no doubt they will do the same. For readers of a younger generation it will be a quite different experience; they will find a largely-disappeared past glowingly revived for them with all its now-faded colours vividly restored. This generation and mine will have comparably good reason to be grateful to the author.

Glanmor Williams
Swansea